Sizzling Sandwiches

Grilled, Wrapped, Stuffed & Stacked

Printed in the United States of America
by G&R Publishing Co.

Distributed By:

507 Industrial Street
Waverly, IA 50677

ISBN-13: 978-1-56383-259-8
ISBN-10: 1-56383-259-3
Item #7023

Table of Contents

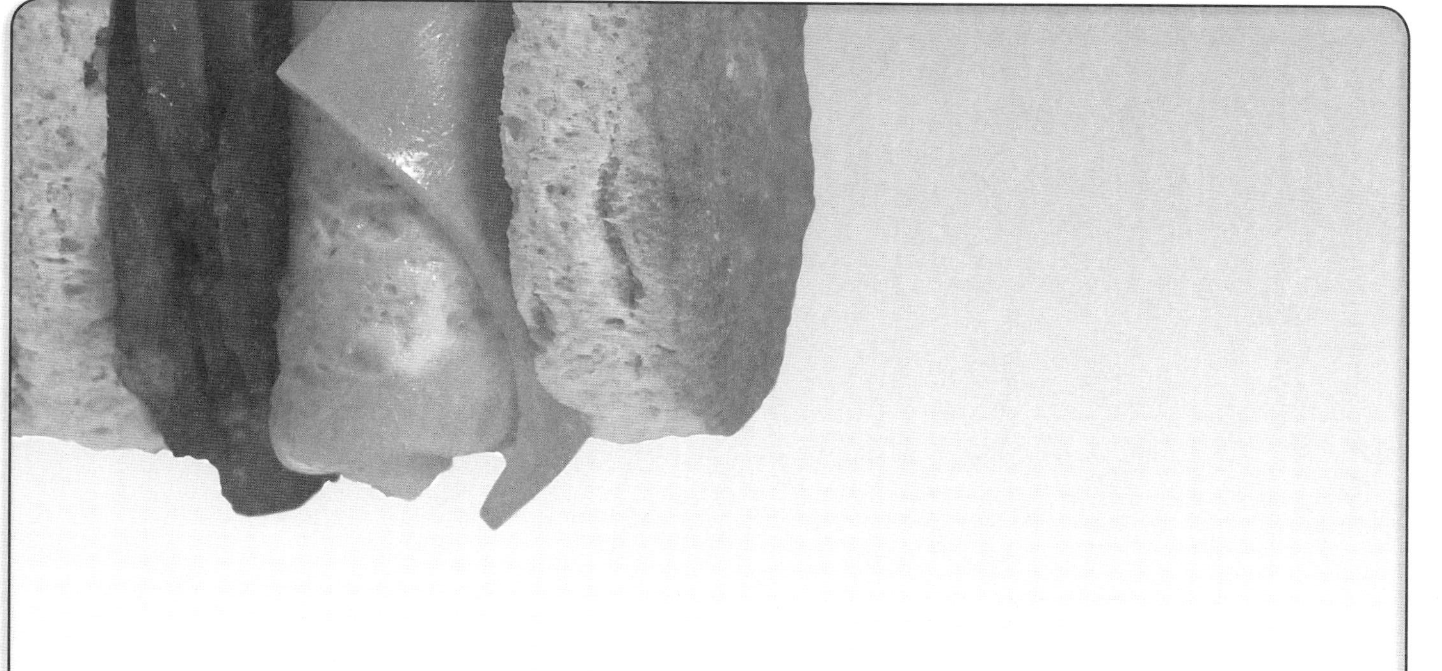

Breakfast

Burritos, Pockets, Quesadillas & Rolls

Tex-Mex Breakfast Burritos

Ingredients

4 slices turkey bacon
2 flour tortillas
2 T. shredded Cheddar cheese
2 large egg whites
1 T. chopped green chiles
Salsa or hot pepper sauce, optional

Directions

In a nonstick skillet over medium heat, cook turkey bacon for 8 to 10 minutes or until browned. Place 2 cooked turkey bacon slices on each tortilla. Sprinkle shredded Cheddar cheese over each tortilla.

In a small bowl, beat together egg whites and chopped green chiles. Add mixture to hot skillet and cook for about 2 minutes, or until eggs are set. Divide scrambled egg mixture between tortillas. Fold tortillas over to enclose filling.

Place one breakfast burrito on each plate and top with salsa, if desired. To keep burritos warm, wrap in aluminum foil and place in warm oven for up to 30 minutes.

Makes 2 servings

BLT Bagel Sandwiches

Ingredients

8 slices bacon
4 plain bagels, split
4 lettuce leaves
4 tomato slices
4 eggs
¼ C. milk
2 tsp. hot pepper sauce
½ C. chopped green peppers

Directions

In a nonstick skillet over medium heat, cook bacon for 8 to 10 minutes or until browned.

Place 1 split bagel on each plate. Cover the bottom half of each bagel with 1 lettuce leaf and 1 tomato slice.

In a small bowl, mix eggs, milk and hot sauce; set aside.

Add chopped green peppers to hot skillet and heat until tender-crisp, about 2 to 3 minutes. Pour egg mixture over green peppers in hot skillet and allow egg mixture to cook without stirring. As eggs set, lift slightly with a spatula to allow uncooked portion of eggs to flow underneath. Continue to cook until egg mixture is completely set.

Top each bagel with ¼ of the cooked egg mixture. Place 2 bacon slices over eggs on each bagel and top with other bagel half.

Makes 4 servings

Sunrise Cinnamon Breakfast Sandwiches

Ingredients

½ C. crunchy peanut butter
8 slices cinnamon raisin bread
4 slices mozzarella cheese
1 red apple, thinly sliced
4 slices Cheddar cheese
Butter

Directions

Spread peanut butter over 4 slices of cinnamon raisin bread; top each with 1 slice of mozzarella cheese, ¼ of the apple slices and 1 Cheddar cheese slice. Cover with remaining bread slices to make 4 sandwiches.

In a large skillet over medium heat, melt butter. Spread butter around skillet and grill sandwiches, 1 or 2 at a time. Continue to grill, turning once, until sandwiches are lightly browned on both sides and cheese is melted. Cut each sandwich in half and serve immediately.

Makes 4 servings

Cheesy Chive Egg Sandwich

2 eggs, beaten
2 T. chive and onion flavored cream cheese
1 English muffin, split and toasted
1 slice American cheese

In a medium skillet over medium heat, cook and stir eggs until set. Stir in cream cheese and continue to heat until cheese is melted and well blended.

Spoon cooked egg mixture onto 1 side of the toasted English muffin. Top with American cheese slice and remaining English muffin, making a sandwich.

Makes 1 serving

Sausage & Cheese Breakfast Burritos

Ingredients

2 lbs. pork sausage
12 eggs, beaten
1 (4 oz.) can chopped green chiles, drained
8 (10″) flour tortillas
2 C. shredded Cheddar cheese
1 tsp. flour
1 C. milk

Directions

Preheat oven to 350°. In a large skillet over medium heat, cook pork sausage until evenly browned. Drain skillet, reserving 2 tablespoons drippings. Set aside cooked sausage.

In a large bowl, beat together eggs and drained green chiles. Add egg mixture to hot skillet and heat, stirring occasionally, until eggs are scrambled and set. Meanwhile, lightly grease a 9 x 13″ baking dish.

Lay out tortillas flat on a cutting board, countertop or table. Cover each tortilla with an even amount of the cooked sausage, shredded Cheddar cheese and cooked egg mixture. Roll up each tortilla and place, seam side down, in the greased baking dish.

Return the reserved sausage drippings to the hot skillet. Sprinkle flour over drippings and stir. Slowly add milk to skillet, stirring constantly, until mixture begins to thicken to gravy. Pour gravy over rolled tortillas in baking dish. Bake in oven for 10 to 15 minutes, or until gravy is bubbly.

Makes 4 to 6 servings

Big Country Biscuit Wraps

Ingredients

1 (12 oz.) tube refrigerated buttermilk biscuits
¾ C. chopped cooked ham
¾ C. shredded Cheddar cheese

Directions

Preheat oven to 400°. Open buttermilk biscuit can and separate dough into 10 biscuits. Press each biscuit into a 5″ round.

Spoon some of the chopped cooked ham and some of the shredded Cheddar cheese over each biscuit. Fold dough in half over filling; press edges with a fork to secure the filling. Place biscuits on an ungreased baking sheet.

Place baking sheet in oven and bake biscuits for 10 to 13 minutes, or until golden brown.

Makes 10 biscuits

Quick 'n Easy Waffle Sandwich

Ingredients

2 frozen waffles
1 T. crunchy peanut butter
2 T. mashed banana
1 tsp. honey

Directions

Toast waffles in a toaster or toaster oven to desired darkness.

In a small bowl, combine crunchy peanut butter, mashed banana and honey. Mix until well combined; spread over waffle and top with second waffle. Serve immediately.

Makes 1 serving

Bacon Egg Pita Pockets

2 pita bread rounds
4 slices bacon
4 eggs
1 T. milk
Salt and pepper to taste
Shredded Cheddar cheese

Cut each pita round in half to form 4 pita pockets. Wrap pita halves in a paper towel and heat in microwave for 10 to 15 seconds.

In a medium skillet over medium-high heat, cook bacon until crisp. Remove bacon from skillet and drain on paper towel. Pour grease from skillet, reserving 1 tablespoon drippings in skillet.

In a medium bowl, whisk together eggs, milk, salt and pepper. Pour egg mixture into skillet and cook, stirring often, until eggs are softly scrambled. Crumble bacon and add to egg mixture in skillet.

Stuff each pita pocket with an even amount of the egg and bacon mixture. Sprinkle some shredded Cheddar cheese over egg mixture in each pita pocket.

Makes 4 servings

Hawaiian-Style Breakfast Wraps

Ingredients

6 eggs
¼ C. milk or water
2 T. butter
¼ C. chopped ham
¼ C. chopped green or red bell pepper
1 (8 oz.) can crushed pineapple, drained
4 flour tortillas

Directions

In a medium bowl, beat together eggs and milk; set aside.

In a large skillet over medium heat, place butter. Once butter is melted, add chopped ham and chopped peppers. Sauté until ham is lightly browned and peppers are tender-crisp. Stir in egg mixture. Add drained crushed pineapple and continue to scramble until egg mixture is set.

Place an even amount of the egg mixture over each tortilla. Roll tortilla to enclose filling and place 1 breakfast wrap on each plate. Serve immediately.

Makes 4 servings

Sunny Salsa Quesadillas

Ingredients

2 slices bacon
1 large egg
Pinch of salt
1 C. shredded cheese, any kind
Vegetable oil
4 (5″) flour tortillas
½ C. salsa
1 C. frozen hash browns, thawed and heated
Diced tomato or avocado, optional

Directions

Cut bacon slices in half. In a medium skillet over medium heat, cook bacon until crisp. Remove bacon, reserving drippings in skillet.

In a small bowl, whisk together egg and salt. Add egg mixture to drippings in skillet. Reduce heat to medium-low and cook until egg mixture just begins to set, about 3 minutes. Stir about 2 tablespoons shredded cheese into egg mixture. Remove skillet from heat.

On a griddle or in the same skillet, place a very thin layer of vegetable oil. Heat oil for about 3 minutes before placing 2 tortillas, side by side, on the griddle. Spread ¼ cup shredded cheese over each tortilla; heat until cheese begins to melt. Quickly spoon about half of the egg mixture onto each tortilla. Top each tortilla with 2 tablespoons salsa, 2 crisp bacon halves and half of the hash browns. If desired, cover with additional cheese or salsa and top with remaining 2 tortillas. Use a wide spatula to quickly flip quesadillas; heat until cheese is melted and tortillas are golden and crisp. Place 1 quesadilla on each plate and, if desired, top with additional shredded cheese, salsa, diced tomato or avocado. Cut each quesadilla into 6 triangles and serve immediately.

Makes 2 servings

Breakfast Sausage Pockets

¼ lb. pork sausage
2 pita bread rounds
3 green onions, chopped
½ tsp. chili powder
6 eggs, lightly beaten
Salsa or shredded cheese, optional

Directions

Preheat oven to 250°. In a medium skillet over medium heat, place crumbled pork sausage. Heat sausage until fully cooked.

Cut each pita bread round in half; wrap in foil and warm in preheated oven for 5 to 10 minutes.

Remove cooked sausage from skillet and drain grease. Return sausage to skillet and add chopped green onions, chili powder and beaten eggs. Heat, stirring often, until eggs are set.

Spoon ¼ of the egg mixture into each pita pocket. If desired, sprinkle salsa or shredded cheese over egg mixture in each serving.

Makes 4 servings

Cheddar Bacon Sandwich Casserole

Ingredients

Butter
16 slices bread, divided
2 C. shredded sharp Cheddar cheese, divided
¾ lb. bacon, diced
1 C. diced onions
¾ C. diced celery
6 T. chopped green peppers
¾ tsp. salt
¾ tsp. pepper
8 tomato slices
6 eggs
3 C. milk
1½ tsp. mustard

Directions

Spread butter over bread slices and trim crust from bread. Arrange 8 slices, buttered side down, in a 9 x 13″ baking dish. Sprinkle 1 cup shredded cheese over bread slices.

In a large skillet over medium high heat, combine diced bacon, diced onions, diced celery, chopped green peppers, salt and pepper, and sauté until tender-crisp. Sprinkle mixture over bread and cheese in baking dish. Arrange tomato slices over bacon mixture. Cover with remaining 8 bread slices, buttered side up.

In a medium bowl, whisk together eggs, milk and mustard. Mix well and pour mixture over bread slices. Top with remaining shredded cheese. Cover baking dish with aluminum foil and place in refrigerator overnight, or for 6 to 8 hours.

Preheat oven to 350°. Remove aluminum foil from baking dish. Bake in oven for 1 hour. To serve, cut casserole into squares and remove from baking dish with a spatula.

Makes 8 to 12 servings

Ham & Swiss Biscuits

Ingredients

2 pkgs. of 12 heat and serve pull-apart rolls
6 slices Swiss cheese
1½ lbs. shaved cooked ham
½ C. butter, melted
1½ T. prepared mustard
1 tsp. Worcestershire sauce
1 T. poppy seeds

Directions

Preheat oven to 350°. Separate rolls into 24 individual biscuits. Cut Swiss cheese slices into quarters. Evenly divide Swiss cheese and ham into 24 portions. Place 1 ham and cheese portion in the center of each roll. Place rolls in a greased 9 x 13″ baking dish.

In a small bowl, combine melted butter, mustard and Worcestershire sauce. Mix well and pour over rolls. Sprinkle poppy seeds over rolls.

Bake in oven for 10 to 15 minutes, or until cheese has melted. To serve, separate rolls with spatula and serve immediately.

Makes 24 small sandwiches

Bacon & Hard-Boiled Egg Sandwiches

Ingredients

¼ C. butter or margarine, softened
8 slices bread
½ C. sour cream
4 green onions, chopped
4 slices American cheese
2 hard-boiled eggs, cut into ¼″ slices
8 slices bacon, cooked, drained and crumbled

Directions

Spread softened butter over 1 side of each bread slice. In a large skillet over medium-high heat, place 4 bread slices, buttered side down. Spread sour cream over bread in skillet. Place chopped green onions, American cheese slices, hard-boiled egg slices and crumbled bacon over sour cream. Top with remaining 4 bread slices, buttered side up.

Continue to heat, turning once, until cheese is melted and sandwiches are grilled and golden brown on both sides. Remove sandwiches from skillet and cut in half. Serve immediately.

Makes 4 servings

Avocado Tortilla Rolls

Ingredients

4 large eggs
1 T. water
1 T. salsa
1 T. butter
1 T. olive oil
2 (6″) corn tortillas, torn into small pieces
¼ C. finely chopped onion
2 T. chopped green chiles
4 flour tortillas
1 medium tomato, chopped
½ C. chopped avocado
2 tsp. minced fresh cilantro
⅔ C. shredded cheese
Sour cream

Directions

In a small bowl, lightly whisk together eggs, water and salsa; set aside.

In a large skillet over medium-high heat, place butter and olive oil. Add torn tortilla pieces and sauté until softened. Add chopped onion and chopped green chiles; sauté until softened.

Pour the egg mixture over ingredients in the hot skillet and cook, stirring often, until eggs are set. Divide mixture evenly onto flour tortillas. Sprinkle chopped tomato, chopped avocado, minced cilantro and shredded cheese over egg mixture in each tortilla. Spread a little sour cream over each serving and roll up tortillas to enclose the filling. Garnish with additional sour cream or salsa.

Makes 4 servings

Burgers

Classic, Turkey, Sausage & Veggie

Family Favorite Burgers

Ingredients

1½ lbs. lean ground beef
¾ C. uncooked old-fashioned oats
½ C. chopped onion or green bell pepper
⅓ C. chili sauce
1 egg
Pinch of seasoned salt
6 hamburger buns, split
6 dill pickles, optional

Directions

Preheat broiler or grill to high heat. In a large bowl, combine ground beef, uncooked oats, chopped onion, chili sauce, egg and seasoned salt. Mix by hand until well combined. Shape mixture into 6 patties.

Place patties on preheated grill, or about 5″ under broiler. Cook burgers for 5 to 6 minutes per side, or until cooked throughout. Place 1 hamburger on each bun. If desired, top with additional chili sauce and dill pickles.

Makes 6 servings

Cheddar Onion Burgers

1 lb. lean ground beef
1 C. shredded Cheddar cheese
¼ C. ketchup
2 T. finely chopped onion
⅛ tsp. pepper
4 hamburger buns, split

Preheat broiler or grill to high heat. In a large bowl, combine ground beef, shredded Cheddar cheese, ketchup, finely chopped onion and pepper. Mix by hand until well combined. Shape mixture into 4 patties.

Place patties on preheated grill, or about 5″ under broiler. Cook burgers for 4 to 5 minutes per side, or until cooked throughout. If desired, toast split buns on grill for 1 to 2 minutes, or place under broiler for 1 minute. Place 1 hamburger on each toasted bun.

Makes 4 servings

Mushroom Bacon Burgers

Ingredients

1 lb. lean ground beef
1 (4 oz.) can mushroom stems and pieces, drained
4 slices bacon, cooked and crumbled
2 T. diced green onions
1 tsp. Worcestershire sauce
1 tsp. soy sauce
½ tsp. salt
4 hamburger buns, split
Tomato slices

Directions

Preheat broiler or grill to high heat. In a large bowl, combine ground beef, drained mushroom pieces, crumbled bacon, diced green onions, Worcestershire sauce, soy sauce and salt. Mix by hand until well combined. Shape mixture into 4 patties.

Place patties on preheated grill, or about 5˝ under broiler. Cook burgers for 4 to 5 minutes per side, or until cooked throughout. Place 1 hamburger on each bun and place 1 or 2 tomato slices over each burger.

Makes 4 servings

Easy Italian Burgers

Ingredients

1 medium onion, chopped
¼ C. Italian salad dressing
1 lb. lean ground beef
4 hamburger buns, split

Directions

Preheat broiler or grill to high heat. In a large bowl, combine chopped onion, Italian dressing and ground beef. Mix by hand until well combined. Shape mixture into 4 patties.

Place patties on preheated grill, or about 5″ under broiler. Cook burgers for 4 to 5 minutes per side, or until cooked throughout. Place 1 hamburger on each bun.

Makes 4 servings

Deluxe Italian Burgers

Ingredients

1 C. dry bread crumbs
¼ C. grated Romano cheese
¼ C. grated Parmesan cheese
1 T. Italian seasoning
1 egg
1 tsp. pepper
1 (6 oz.) can tomato paste
½ lb. ground Italian sausage
1 lb. lean ground beef
8 hamburger buns, split
8 slices Provolone cheese

Directions

Preheat broiler or grill to high heat. In a large bowl, combine dry bread crumbs, grated Romano cheese, grated Parmesan cheese and Italian seasoning. Add egg, pepper, tomato paste, ground Italian sausage and ground beef. Mix by hand until well combined. Shape mixture into 8 patties.

Place patties on preheated grill, or about 5″ under broiler. Cook burgers for about 5 minutes per side, or until cooked throughout. Be sure to watch doneness of burgers, as the tomato paste will tint the meat red even when well cooked. Place 1 hamburger on each bun. Top each burger with 1 slice Provolone cheese and serve.

Makes 8 servings

Swiss Brew Burgers

¼ C. Heinz 57 sauce
¼ C. beer
1 large sweet onion
1½ lbs. lean ground beef
6 slices Swiss cheese
6 white or whole wheat rolls, split
Lettuce leaves

In a glass measuring cup, combine Heinz 57 sauce and beer. Mix well and place in microwave. Cook for 1 to 1½ minutes, or until mixture bubbles; set aside.

Cut onion into ½″ slices. Shape ground beef into 6 patties. Place onion slices in a large skillet over medium heat, or on a lightly-oiled grate over a preheated grill. Grill or sauté onions for 5 minutes. Place patties in skillet or over grill and heat for about 6 minutes per side, or until cooked throughout.

Approximately 2 minutes before burgers are done, brush sauce generously over patties. Place 1 Swiss cheese slice over each burger. Once cheese has melted, place 1 burger on each roll. Top each burger with some of the grilled onions and a few lettuce leaves.

Makes 6 servings

Zesty Turkey Burgers

½ onion, minced
2 T. chopped red bell pepper
1 lb. ground turkey
⅓ C. dry bread crumbs
2 T. chicken broth
2 cloves garlic, minced
1 jalapeno pepper, minced
½ tsp. dried oregano
½ tsp. salt
½ tsp. pepper
2 T. olive oil
4 hamburger buns, split
½ C. salsa

Directions

In a small skillet over medium-high heat, sauté minced onion and chopped red bell pepper until softened.

In a large bowl, combine cooked onion and green bell pepper, ground turkey, dry bread crumbs, chicken broth, minced garlic, minced jalapeno pepper, dried oregano, salt and pepper. Mix by hand until well combined. Form mixture into 4 patties.

In a large skillet over medium-high heat, place olive oil. Sauté turkey burgers in pan for 4 to 5 minutes per side, or until cooked throughout. Place 1 turkey burger on each bun and top each with 2 tablespoons salsa.

Makes 4 servings

Turkey Salsa Burgers

Ingredients

1 egg
Salt and pepper to taste
1¼ lbs. ground turkey
½ C. flour
1 T. unsalted butter
2 T. vegetable oil
4 hamburger buns, split
½ C. salsa
¼ C. fresh chopped cilantro

Directions

In a large bowl, whisk together egg, salt and pepper. Add ground turkey and mix until just combined. Form mixture into 4 patties, each about ¾" thick.

In a shallow bowl, combine flour and additional salt and pepper. Dredge patties in flour mixture. In a large skillet over medium-high heat, place butter and vegetable oil. Once butter is melted, place burgers in skillet and cook for about 5 minutes per side, or until cooked throughout. The turkey should be white but still juicy.

Remove burgers from skillet and place on paper towels to drain. Place 1 turkey burger on each bun. Top each burger with some of the salsa and 1 tablespoon fresh chopped cilantro.

Makes 4 servings

Tangy Horseradish Hamburgers

Ingredients

1 lb. lean ground beef or turkey
4 tsp. prepared horseradish
2 tsp. Dijon mustard
1 tsp. paprika
¼ tsp. pepper
⅛ tsp. salt
4 hamburger buns, split

Directions

Preheat broiler or grill to high heat. In a large bowl, combine ground beef, prepared horseradish, Dijon mustard, paprika, pepper and salt. Mix by hand until well combined. Shape mixture into 4 patties.

Place patties on preheated grill, or about 5″ under broiler. Cook burgers for about 5 minutes per side, or until cooked throughout. Place 1 hamburger on each bun.

Makes 4 servings

Pizzazzy Pizza Burgers

Ingredients

1 lb. lean ground beef
½ lb. Italian sausage
¼ C. diced green onion
¼ C. diced green bell pepper
1 C. diced tomato
1 (4 oz.) can sliced olives, drained
6 hamburger buns, split
6 slices cheese, any kind
1½ C. pizza sauce
Grated Parmesan cheese

Directions

In a medium bowl, mix together ground beef and Italian sausage by hand. Form mixture into 6 patties. In a large skillet over medium-high heat, cook burgers, turning once, until cooked throughout.

In small bowl, toss together diced green onion, diced green bell pepper, diced tomato and drained olives. Mix until well combined.

Spread butter over buns and place under broiler for 1 to 2 minutes, or until buns are lightly toasted. Place 1 hamburger on each bun and top each with 1 slice of cheese. Spread about ¼ cup pizza sauce over cheese on each burger. Place a spoonful of the vegetable mixture over pizza sauce and sprinkle with grated Parmesan cheese.

Makes 6 servings

Double Deluxe Cheeseburgers

Ingredients

1 egg
1 (6 oz.) can tomato paste
1 T. Worcestershire sauce
1 medium onion, chopped
½ C. grated Parmesan cheese
½ tsp. seasoned salt
½ tsp. salt
⅛ tsp. pepper
2 lbs. lean ground beef
8 slices Cheddar cheese
8 hamburger buns, split

Directions

Preheat grill to medium heat. In a large bowl, combine egg, tomato paste, Worcestershire sauce, chopped onion, grated Parmesan cheese, seasoned salt, salt and pepper. Crumble ground beef into bowl and mix by hand until well combined. Shape mixture into 8 patties, each about ¾″ thick.

Place burgers on preheated grill. Cover grill and cook for 5 minutes on each side. Top each burger with 1 slice Cheddar cheese. Grill for an additional 1 to 2 minutes, or until cheese is melted. Place 1 hamburger on each bun.

Makes 8 servings

Herbed Swiss Burgers

1½ lbs. lean ground beef
Salt and pepper to taste
¼ C. unsalted butter, softened
1 T. fresh chopped parsley
½ tsp. dried tarragon
½ tsp. dried basil
1 red onion, sliced
6 slices Swiss cheese
6 English muffins, split

Preheat broiler or grill to high heat. In a medium bowl, combine ground beef, salt and pepper to taste; mix well. Shape ground beef into 6 patties. In a small bowl, combine softened butter, fresh chopped parsley, dried tarragon and dried basil; set aside. In a small skillet over medium-high heat, sauté red onion slices until softened.

Place patties on preheated grill, or about 5″ under broiler. Cook burgers for 4 to 5 minutes per side, or until cooked throughout. Top each burger with 1 slice Swiss cheese and grill for an additional 30 seconds to 1 minute, or until cheese is melted.

Toast each English muffin half and spread some of the butter mixture over each half. Place some of the sautéed onions on 6 of the English muffin halves. Place 1 burger over onions on English muffins and top with remaining 6 English muffin halves.

Makes 6 servings

Burgundy Burgers

1½ lbs. lean ground beef
Seasoned salt to taste
1 to 2 C. Burgundy wine
6 slices American or Swiss cheese
6 hamburger buns, split

Directions

Preheat broiler or grill to high heat. Shape ground beef into 4 patties. Place patties on preheated grill, or about 5″ under broiler. Sprinkle patties lightly with seasoned salt. Cook burgers for about 3 minutes per side. Carefully pour ¼ cup to ½ cup Burgundy wine on each patty and heat for a few minutes more, or until cooked to desired doneness.

Top each burger with 1 slice American or Swiss cheese. Place 1 hamburger on each bun.

Makes 6 servings

French Dijon Burgers

Ingredients

1½ lbs. lean ground beef
3 T. Dijon mustard
1 T. fresh minced thyme
1 T. white wine
2 T. minced dried onion
2 cloves garlic, minced
6 hamburger buns, split

Directions

Preheat broiler. In a large bowl, combine ground beef, Dijon mustard, minced thyme, white wine, minced dried onion and minced garlic. Mix by hand until well combined. Shape mixture into 6 patties.

Place burger on broiler pan and place pan about 5″ under broiler. Cook burgers to desired doneness (3 to 4 minutes for rare, 5 to 7 minutes for medium, 8 to 9 minutes for well-done). Place 1 hamburger on each bun.

Makes 6 servings

Guacamole Monterey Burgers

Ingredients

1½ lbs. lean ground beef
1 (2 oz.) piece Monterey Jack cheese, quartered
4 tsp. finely chopped pickled jalapeno peppers, optional
Salt and pepper to taste
1 avocado
2½ tsp. lemon juice
⅓ C. finely diced tomato
3 T. minced green onion
¼ tsp. ground cumin
2 T. fresh chopped cilantro
4 hamburger buns, split

Directions

Divide the ground beef into parts and shape each part into a ball. Make an indentation in the center of each ball and stuff each with 1 small piece of Monterey Jack cheese and 1 teaspoon finely chopped jalapeno peppers. Form the ground beef around the filling and press each ball into a 1″ thick patty. Season the burgers with salt and pepper to taste. Grill burgers in a large skillet for about 5 minutes on each side, or to desired doneness.

While the burgers are grilling, prepare the guacamole. Halve, pit and peel the avocado. In a medium bowl, mash the avocado flesh with a fork. Stir in lemon juice, diced tomato, minced green onion, cumin and cilantro. Mix until well combined and season with salt and pepper to taste.

Place 1 hamburger on each bun and top with a generous amount of the guacamole. Top with bun tops and serve immediately.

Makes 4 servings

Spicy Bean Burgers

Ingredients

1 (16 oz.) can red kidney beans, drained and mashed
1 carrot, steamed and mashed
½ C. coarsely chopped onion
½ green pepper, coarsely chopped
2 T. salsa
1 C. dry bread crumbs
½ C. flour
½ to 1 tsp. pepper
Dash of chili powder
8 to 10 hamburger buns, split

Directions

Preheat oven to 450°. Mash the beans and carrot and chop the onion and green pepper. In a large bowl, combine mashed kidney beans, mashed carrot, chopped onion, chopped green pepper, salsa, dry bread crumbs, flour, pepper and chili powder. If mixture is too runny, add a little more flour. If mixture is too stiff, add a little more salsa.

Form mixture into 8 to 10 balls; flatten balls into patties. Place burgers on a baking sheet and bake in oven for about 15 to 20 minutes, or until browned and cooked throughout. Place 1 hamburger on each bun.

Makes 8 to 10 servings

All-American Burgers

Ingredients

½ C. mayonnaise
½ tsp. garlic powder
½ tsp. onion powder
1 lb. lean ground beef
2 T. dry bread crumbs
Salt and pepper to taste
4 slices American cheese
8 lettuce leaves
4 hamburger buns, split
1 tomato, sliced

Directions

Preheat grill to high heat and lightly oil the grate. In a large bowl, combine mayonnaise, garlic powder and onion powder. Transfer ¼ cup of the mayonnaise mixture to a second bowl. To this, add ground beef, dry bread crumbs, salt and pepper. Mix by hand until well combined. Shape mixture into 4 patties, each about ½″ thick.

Place patties on lightly oiled grate and grill for about 3 to 4 minutes per side, or until cooked throughout. Top each patty with 1 American cheese slice and continue to heat until cheese begins to melt.

Spread buns with reserved mayonnaise mixture and top each with a few lettuce leaves. Place 1 hamburger on each bun and top with tomato slices.

Makes 4 servings

Chili Beer Burgers

2 lbs. lean ground beef
Pepper to taste
1 T. hot pepper sauce
1 clove garlic, crushed
⅓ C. chili sauce
½ pkg. dry onion soup mix
½ C. beer, divided
8 hamburger buns, split

Preheat oven to 400°. In a large bowl, combine ground beef, pepper, hot pepper sauce, crushed garlic, chili sauce, dry onion soup mix and ¼ cup beer. Mix by hand until well combined. Shape mixture into 8 patties.

Place patties on a baking sheet and bake in oven for about 10 minutes. Baste burgers with remaining beer and continue to bake for an additional 10 to 15 minutes, or until cooked throughout. Place 1 hamburger on each bun.

Makes 8 servings

Old-Fashioned Barbecued Burgers

Ingredients

1½ lbs. lean ground beef
¾ C. uncooked old-fashioned oats
3 T. dried minced onion
1 C. milk
Salt and pepper to taste
2 C. ketchup
6 T. apple cider vinegar
4 T. Worcestershire sauce
4 T. sugar
1 C. water
6 hamburger buns, split

Directions

Preheat oven to 325°. In a large bowl, combine ground beef, uncooked oats, dried minced onion, milk, salt and pepper. Mix by hand until well combined. Shape mixture into 6 patties. Place patties in a baking dish or roasting pan.

In a medium bowl, combine ketchup, apple cider vinegar, Worcestershire sauce, sugar and water. Mix until well combined; pour over patties in baking dish.

Bake hamburgers in oven for 1 hour to 1 hour and 30 minutes. Place 1 hamburger on each bun.

Makes 6 servings

Saucy Veggie Burgers

Ingredients

1 (10 oz.) pkg. frozen chopped spinach
1 medium onion, finely chopped
1 medium green bell pepper, finely chopped
1 large potato, cooked, peeled and finely chopped
1 C. French-style cut frozen green beans, thawed
1 T. garlic powder
1 T. dried minced onions
½ tsp. paprika
½ C. barbecue sauce
½ C. dry bread crumbs
1½ C. uncooked old-fashioned oats
½ tsp. seasoned salt
1 tsp. vegetable broth powder
Oil
12 to 15 hamburger buns, split

Directions

Thaw package of frozen chopped spinach in the microwave and squeeze all the liquid from the packet. Place thawed spinach on paper towels and squeeze to remove any excess liquid. In a medium skillet over medium-high heat, sauté finely chopped onion and green bell pepper until softened.

In a large bowl, combine drained spinach, chopped cooked potato, sautéed onion and sautéed green bell pepper. Add thawed green beans, garlic powder, dried minced onions, paprika, barbecue sauce, dry bread crumbs, uncooked oats, seasoned salt and vegetable broth powder. Mix by hand until well combined. Form mixture into 12 to 15 thin patties.

In a large skillet or frying pan, place a thin layer of oil. Fry patties in oil, turning once, until heated throughout. Place 1 veggie burger on each bun.

Makes 12 to 15 servings

Loaded Veggie Burgers

Ingredients

2 tsp. olive oil
1 C. finely chopped onion
1 C. coarsely grated carrots
1 C. coarsely grated zucchini
½ C. coarsely grated beets
2 cloves garlic, minced
½ tsp. ground cumin
½ C. uncooked instant rolled oats
1½ C. mashed potatoes
½ C. cooked rice
1 T. fresh minced dill, tarragon or basil
Salt and pepper to taste
8 hamburger buns, split

Directions

In a large skillet over medium heat, place olive oil. Add chopped onion, grated carrots, grated zucchini, grated beets, minced garlic and ground cumin. Sauté mixture until vegetables are tender and liquid has evaporated, about 10 to 15 minutes. Meanwhile, soak the uncooked oats in ½ cup water for 5 minutes; drain.

Stir the drained oats into the sautéed mixture. Add mashed potatoes, cooked rice, fresh minced dill, and salt and pepper. Mix until well combined. Remove mixture from heat and let cool for a few minutes before shaping mixture into 8 thick patties. Place patties on a plate, cover with plastic wrap and chill in refrigerator at least 3 hours.

Preheat broiler. Cover a broiler pan with aluminum foil; spray with non-stick cooking spray. Place burgers on foil and place broiler pan 5″ to 6″ below heat. Cook veggie burgers for 4 to 6 minutes per side, gently turning burgers over with a spatula. Place 1 veggie burger on each bun.

Makes 8 servings

Hot Dogs
Wrapped, On a Stick & Fully-Loaded

Chicago-Style Dogs

Ingredients

10 beef hot dogs
10 poppy seed hot dog buns
Yellow mustard
Sweet pickle relish
Chopped onions
Kosher dill pickle spears
Sliced tomatoes
Serrano peppers, seeded and sliced
Celery salt

Directions

In a large pot of boiling water, cook hot dogs until heated and cooked throughout. If using a grill, cook hot dogs until internal temperature reaches 170°. Place 1 cooked hot dog on each poppy seed bun.

Pile the following toppings on each hot dog in this order: 1 teaspoon yellow mustard, 1 teaspoon sweet pickle relish, 1 teaspoon chopped onions, 1 dill pickle spear, 2 tomato slices, 2 Serrano pepper slices and a dash of celery salt.

Makes 10 servings

Coney Island Franks

Ingredients

8 beef hot dogs
⅓ C. sweet pickle relish
2 T. sweet pickle liquid
1 T. margarine, melted
1 tsp. yellow mustard
⅛ tsp. pepper
⅛ tsp. onion salt
⅛ tsp. garlic salt
8 hot dog buns

Directions

Cut a deep slit lengthwise into each hot dog, making sure not to cut all the way through. Stuff each hot dog with some of the sweet pickle relish and fasten closed with wooden toothpicks.

In a small bowl, combine sweet pickle liquid, melted margarine, yellow mustard, pepper, onion salt and garlic salt. Brush liquid mixture over hot dogs.

Heat hot dogs over an outdoor grill for 5 to 7 minutes, brushing additional liquid over hot dogs as they cook. To serve, place 1 cooked hot dog on each bun.

Makes 8 servings

Pigs in a Blanket

Ingredients

2 C. biscuit baking mix
½ C. milk
12 hot dogs
2 T. butter or margarine, melted

Directions

Preheat oven to 325°. In a medium bowl, combine biscuit baking mix and milk. Mix until well combined and turn dough out onto a lightly floured flat surface.

Knead dough and pat into a 12″ square. Cut the square into 12 (3 x 4″) pieces. Wrap one square dough piece around each hot dog and pinch to seal. Brush melted butter over dough and hot dogs.

Place wrapped hot dogs on an ungreased baking sheet. Bake in oven for about 10 minutes, or until dough is golden brown and hot dogs are heated through.

Makes 12 servings

Classic Corn Dogs

Ingredients

1 C. flour
2 T. sugar
1½ tsp. baking powder
1 tsp. salt
⅔ C. cornmeal
2 T. shortening
1 egg, lightly beaten
¾ C. milk
10 wooden popsicle sticks
10 hot dogs
Vegetable oil for frying

Directions

Into a medium bowl, sift flour, sugar, baking powder and salt. Stir in cornmeal. Using a pastry blender, cut in shortening, mixing until dough resembles coarse crumbs. In a small bowl, combine egg and milk. Stir milk mixture into flour mixture until well blended.

Insert 1 wooden popsicle stick into 1 end of each hot dog. Dip the hot dogs, one at a time, into the batter until evenly coated, shaking to remove any excess. Fry the corn dogs in the hot oil until evenly browned. Set corn dogs on paper towels to drain.

Makes 10 servings

Easy Crescent Dogs

8 hot dogs
4 American cheese singles
1 (8 oz.) tube crescent rolls

Preheat oven to 375°. Cut a deep slit lengthwise into each hot dog to within ½″ of each end, making sure not to cut all the way through. Slice each of the American cheese singles into 4 strips. Insert 2 cheese strips into the pocket in each hot dog.

Separate the crescent roll dough into triangles. Wrap 1 triangle around each hot dog, enclosing the cheese. Place the wrapped hot dogs on an ungreased baking sheet. Bake in oven for 12 minutes, or until crescent rolls are golden brown.

Makes 8 servings

Barbecue Franks

Ingredients

10 hot dogs
1½ T. Worcestershire sauce
¼ C. vinegar
1 to 2 T. sugar
½ C. ketchup
½ C. water
½ C. chopped onions
½ C. chopped green bell pepper
10 hot dog buns

Directions

Preheat oven to 350°. In a 9 x 13″ baking dish, place hot dogs. In a medium bowl, combine Worcestershire sauce, vinegar, sugar, ketchup, water, chopped onions and chopped green bell pepper. Mix until well combined.

Pour mixture over hot dogs in baking dish; spread evenly. Bake in oven for 1 hour.

To serve, carefully remove hot dogs from baking dish. Place 1 hot dog on each bun. Spread any additional toppings from baking dish over hot dogs.

Makes 10 servings

Saucy Hot Dogs

Ingredients

1 C. finely chopped onion
2 cloves garlic, minced
4 T. butter
½ tsp. salt
⅛ tsp. pepper
1½ T. yellow mustard
1½ T. Worcestershire sauce
1½ tsp. sugar
½ C. chili sauce
10 to 12 hot dogs
10 to 12 hot dog buns

Directions

Preheat broiler. In a small saucepan over medium heat, sauté chopped onion and minced garlic in butter. Continue to heat, stirring often, until onions and garlic are tender, about 10 minutes.

Add salt, pepper, yellow mustard, Worcestershire sauce, sugar and chili sauce to saucepan. Cook, stirring often, for an additional 5 minutes.

Meanwhile, cut a deep slit lengthwise into each hot dog, making sure not to cut all the way through. Spoon an even amount of the onion mixture into the hot dogs. Place the stuffed hot dogs, split-side up, in a 9 x 13″ baking dish. Place baking dish 5″ under broiler and heat for 3 to 5 minutes, until sauce is bubbly.

To serve, place 1 stuffed hot dog on each bun. If desired, spoon any additional sauce from baking dish over hot dogs.

Makes 10 to 12 servings

Wraps
Rolled & Folded

BLT Roll-Ups

Ingredients

3 C. shredded lettuce
1½ C. fresh diced tomatoes
12 strips bacon, cooked and crumbled
¼ C. mayonnaise
⅛ tsp. pepper
4 (10″) flour tortillas

Directions

In a large bowl, combine shredded lettuce, diced tomatoes, crumbled bacon, mayonnaise and pepper. Mix until well combined.

Spoon mixture down the center of each tortilla. Fold sides up, rolling to enclose the filling. Serve immediately.

Makes 4 servings

Deli Roast Beef Sandwich Rolls

Ingredients

2 (1 lb.) loaves frozen bread dough, thawed
¾ C. chopped sweet red pepper
½ C. chopped red onion
1 tsp. garlic salt
1 tsp. Italian seasoning
8 oz. thinly sliced deli roast beef
2 C. finely shredded Cheddar cheese
1 egg white
1 T. water

Directions

Once bread dough has thawed, combine the 2 loaves and shape into a ball. Place the ball of dough in a greased bowl, turning once to grease the top of the dough. Cover the bowl with a towel and let the dough rise in a warm place for 90 minutes.

Preheat oven to 400°. In a microwave-safe bowl, combine the chopped red pepper, chopped red onion, garlic salt and Italian seasoning. Cover bowl and microwave on high for 1 minute, or until vegetables are tender.

Punch down the dough and transfer to a lightly floured flat surface. Roll dough into a 12 x 15″ rectangle. Cut the sliced roast beef into long, thin strips. In a medium bowl, combine the roast beef strips, shredded Cheddar cheese and red pepper mixture; toss until well combined. Spread the beef mixture over the dough to within ½″ from the edge. Roll up the dough into a long roll, starting at the long end. Pinch the ends to seal the filling. Place the roll, seam-side down, on a lightly greased baking sheet.

In a small bowl, beat together the egg white and water. Use a pastry brush to spread egg wash over the dough. Use a sharp knife to cut a long slit in top of the dough. Bake in oven for 30 to 35 minutes, or until golden brown. Remove from oven and let stand for 10 minutes before slicing into rounds.

Makes 8 servings

Reuben Square Roll-Ups

Ingredients

1 (14 oz.) pkg. refrigerated pizza dough
1 C. sauerkraut, drained
1 T. thousand island salad dressing
4 slices corned beef, halved
4 slices Swiss cheese, halved

Directions

Roll out dough into a 9 x 12″ rectangle. Cut dough into 8 (3 x 4½″) rectangles. In a small bowl, combine sauerkraut and salad dressing; mix well.

Place 1 slice of corned beef on each rectangle. Top corned beef on each rectangle with 2 tablespoons of the sauerkraut mixture and 1 slice of Swiss cheese. Roll up each rectangle and place, seam-side down, on a greased baking sheet. Bake in oven for 12 to 14 minutes, or until dough is golden brown.

Makes 8 servings

Fabulous Burger Wraps

Ingredients

1½ lbs. lean ground beef
Salt and pepper to taste
6 slices provolone or Cheddar cheese
¼ C. plus 2 T. roasted red bell peppers,
  drained and chopped
1 (6 oz.) jar marinated artichokes,
  drained and chopped
2 T. unsalted butter
2 T. Worcestershire sauce
6 (8″) flour tortillas, warmed
Ranch salad dressing

Directions

Shape ground beef into 12 flat patties; season with salt and pepper to taste. On 6 of the patties, place 1 cheese slice, a spoonful of the chopped roasted red peppers and a spoonful of the chopped artichokes. Cover with remaining patties and pinch the edges together to enclose the filling.

In a heavy skillet over medium heat, combine butter and Worcestershire sauce, mixing until butter is completely melted. Arrange burgers in skillet and sauté for about 10 minutes, turning occasionally until cooked throughout. Transfer cooked burgers to a plate and keep warm. Spread mayonnaise over each tortilla and place 1 burger on each tortilla. Fold tortilla up and over to enclose each burger. Serve immediately.

Makes 6 servings

Beef Salsa Wraps

Ingredients

½ C. sour cream
¼ C. mayonnaise
3 T. salsa
10 (8″) flour tortillas, warmed
1 lb. deli roast beef
10 large lettuce leaves

Directions

In a small bowl, combine sour cream, mayonnaise and salsa; mix until well combined. Spread mixture over warmed tortillas.

Divide the roast beef slices evenly over each tortilla. Place 1 lettuce leaf over roast beef on each tortilla. Roll up tortillas to enclose the filling. If necessary, secure wraps with toothpicks. Cut each roll in half and, if desired, serve with additional salsa.

Makes 10 servings

Oriental Steak Wraps

1 C. rice vinegar
2 T. sesame oil
1 T. honey
1½ lbs. beef flank steak or top sirloin
2 C. cole slaw
½ C. chopped green onions
Salt and pepper to taste
6 (10″) flour tortillas, warmed
⅓ C. honey roasted peanuts, optional

In a small bowl, whisk together rice vinegar, sesame oil and honey until well combined. Place beef steak in a large plastic bag and add ¾ cup of the honey mixture. Close bag tightly, squeezing gently to remove any air from the bag. Place bag in refrigerator, allowing steak to marinate for 10 minutes.

Meanwhile, in a medium bowl, combine cole slaw, chopped green onions, salt, pepper and remaining honey mixture; toss until well combined. Remove steak from refrigerator and discard marinade.

Preheat grill. Grill steak, uncovered, over medium heat for 17 to 20 minutes, or until steaks are cooked to desired doneness. Remove steak from grill and carve into thin slices. Season the steak slices with salt and pepper to taste.

Layer an even amount of the steak slices down the center of each tortilla. Divide the cole slaw evenly over the steak slices on each tortilla. Sprinkle an even amount of the peanuts over each serving. Roll up the sandwiches by folding in the edges and rolling to enclose the ingredients. Serve immediately.

Makes 6 servings

Turkey Ranch Veggie Wraps

4 (8″) flour tortillas
4 T. salsa, divided
4 T. ranch salad dressing, divided
24 spinach leaves
4 turkey breast slices
4 tsp. chopped red onion, divided
4 tsp. chopped red bell peppers, divided
4 tsp. chopped zucchini, divided
1 C. shredded mozzarella cheese, divided

Directions

Place the tortillas on a flat surface. Spread 1 tablespoon salsa and 1 tablespoon ranch dressing over each tortilla. Divide spinach leaves evenly over the tortillas. Place 1 turkey slice over the spinach leaves on each tortilla. Add 1 teaspoon chopped red onion, 1 teaspoon chopped bell pepper and 1 teaspoon chopped zucchini over each tortilla. Gently press down on the ingredients.

Sprinkle ¼ cup shredded mozzarella cheese on each serving. Roll up the sandwiches by folding in the edges and rolling to enclose the ingredients. Serve immediately.

Makes 4 servings

Spicy Chicken Wraps

Ingredients

1 C. chopped onion
1 C. sliced green bell pepper
1 small jalapeno pepper, seeded and minced
1 tsp. minced garlic
2 tsp. vegetable oil
½ lb. boneless, skinless chicken breasts,
   cut into thin strips
1 lb. black beans, drained and rinsed
1 lb. canned refried beans, warmed
6 (10″) flour tortillas
¼ C. plus 2 T. salsa
¼ C. plus 2 T. sour cream

Directions

In a large skillet over medium heat, sauté chopped onion, sliced green bell pepper, minced jalapeno and minced garlic in vegetable oil. Heat, stirring often, for 2 to 3 minutes. Cover skillet and heat for an additional 2 to 3 minutes.

Add chicken strips to skillet and heat for 5 minutes, or until chicken is cooked throughout. Add drained black beans and continue to heat for 1 to 2 minutes, or until mixture is warmed.

Spread about ⅓ cup refried beans in the center of each tortilla. Spoon about half of the chicken mixture over the refried beans on each tortilla. Spoon a little salsa and a little sour cream over each tortilla. Roll up the sandwiches by folding in the edges and rolling to enclose the ingredients. Serve immediately.

Makes 6 servings

Herbed Turkey Roll-Ups

Ingredients

1 (8 oz.) pkg. cream cheese, softened
½ C. mayonnaise
¼ tsp. dried basil
¼ tsp. dried oregano
¼ tsp. dried dillweed
¼ tsp. garlic powder
10 (6") flour tortillas, warmed
1 medium onion, chopped
10 slices deli sliced turkey
Shredded lettuce

Directions

In a small bowl, combine cream cheese, mayonnaise, dried basil, dried oregano, dried dillweed and garlic powder. Mix until well combined. Spread mixture over each tortilla.

Sprinkle chopped onion over herbed mixture. Divide turkey slices over tortillas and sprinkle shredded lettuce over each. Roll up tightly to enclose the filling. If necessary, secure with toothpicks. Serve immediately.

Makes 10 servings

Fiesta Veggie Wraps

Ingredients

1 (8 oz.) pkg. cream cheese, softened
½ C. sour cream
1 (4 oz.) can chopped green chiles, drained
1 T. taco seasoning
4 (10″) flour tortillas, warmed
2 avocados, peeled, pitted and sliced
2 plum tomatoes, thinly sliced
5 green onions, sliced
1 (4 oz.) can sliced olives, drained

Directions

In a small bowl, combine cream cheese, sour cream, drained green chiles and taco seasoning; mix until well combined. Spread about ½ cup of the cream cheese mixture in an even layer over each tortilla.

Place a few avocado slices, a few tomato slices and a few onion slices over each tortilla. Sprinkle a few sliced olives over each serving. Roll up tightly to enclose the filling. If necessary, secure with toothpicks. Serve immediately.

Makes 4 servings

Cheddar Chicken Wraps

Ingredients

1 lb. boneless, skinless chicken breasts, cut into 1″ cubes
¼ C. chopped onion
¼ tsp. ground cumin
1 T. butter or margarine
¼ C. chopped pecans
3 T. sour cream
4 (10″) flour tortillas, warmed
1 C. shredded Cheddar cheese
1 C. salsa
Shredded lettuce

Directions

In a large skillet over medium heat, sauté cubed chicken, chopped onion and ground cumin in butter. Heat until chicken is cooked throughout. Reduce heat to low and add chopped pecans and sour cream. Continue to cook, stirring often, until heated throughout.

Spoon about ½ cup of the mixture down the center of each tortilla. Sprinkle an even amount of shredded Cheddar cheese, salsa and shredded lettuce over the chicken mixture in each tortilla. Fold in sides and roll to enclose the filling. Serve immediately.

Makes 4 servings

Deluxe Sloppy Joe Wraps

Ingredients

4 (10″) flour tortillas
¾ lb. lean ground beef
½ lb. crumbled Italian sausage
2 C. canned sloppy joe sauce
2 C. cooked white rice
½ C. sliced green onions
½ C. sour cream

Directions

Preheat oven to 200°. Wrap tortillas in aluminum foil and place in oven to keep warm.

In a large skillet over medium-high heat, sauté ground beef and crumbled Italian sausage for 7 to 8 minutes, or until meat is browned. Stir in sloppy joe sauce, cooked white rice and sliced green onions, mixing until well blended.

Remove warmed tortillas from oven and spread sour cream evenly over each. Spoon the meat and rice mixture over the sour cream. Fold in sides and roll to enclose the filling. Serve immediately.

Makes 4 servings

Tangy Garden Wraps

Ingredients

1 C. chopped tomatoes
1 C. chopped zucchinis
1 C. chopped yellow squash
1 C. chopped red bell peppers
1 C. cooked brown rice
½ tsp. garlic powder
½ tsp. dried oregano
½ tsp. lime juice
2 T. balsamic vinegar
⅛ tsp. hot pepper sauce
4 (8″) flour tortillas, warmed

Directions

Preheat broiler. On a large baking sheet or jellyroll pan, spread out chopped tomatoes, chopped zucchinis, chopped yellow squash and chopped red bell peppers in an even layer. Place under broiler for about 5 to 10 minutes, or until vegetables are softened and browned. In a large bowl, combine softened vegetables, cooked brown rice, garlic powder, dried oregano, lime juice, balsamic vinegar and hot pepper sauce; mix until well combined.

Place the tortillas on a flat surface. Spread about 1 cup of the vegetable mixture down the center of each tortilla. Fold in sides and roll to enclose the filling. Serve immediately.

Makes 4 servings

Stuffed

Pockets, Turnovers, Quesadillas & Pitas

Deluxe Stuffed Pizza Wedges

Ingredients

1 loaf frozen bread dough, thawed
¼ lb. deli salami, chopped
¼ lb. deli pepperoni, chopped
¼ lb. prosciutto or ham, chopped
½ C. sliced onions, sautéed
½ C. shredded mozzarella cheese
½ C. shredded milk Cheddar cheese
2 cloves garlic, minced
2 T. fresh chopped parsley
2 T. fresh chopped basil
1 T. fresh chopped oregano
¼ tsp. red pepper flakes
2 tsp. olive oil

Directions

Preheat oven to 400°. Divide bread dough in half. Roll out half of the dough into a 12˝ circle and press into a 12˝ greased pizza pan. In a medium bowl, combine the chopped salami, chopped pepperoni, chopped prosciutto, sautéed onions, shredded mozzarella cheese, shredded Cheddar cheese, minced garlic, parsley, basil, oregano and red pepper flakes; toss until well combined. Spread mixture out over pizza dough in pan.

Roll the remaining half of dough into a 12˝ circle and place over the filling in the pan. Pinch the 2 dough edges together to enclose the filling. Use a pastry brush to spread olive oil over the dough, cutting a slit in the top of the dough for steam to escape. Bake in oven for 15 minutes, or until dough is puffy and golden brown. Remove from oven and let cool slightly before cutting into wedges and serving.

Makes 4 servings

Ham 'n Broccoli Pockets

2 C. broccoli florets
1½ C. shredded sharp Cheddar cheese
½ C. cooked cubed ham
½ C. sliced green onions
1 T. fresh minced parsley
¼ tsp. nutmeg
Salt and pepper to taste
Pastry for double-crust pie
1 egg
1 T. heavy whipping cream

Directions

Preheat oven to 400°. Place broccoli florets in a steamer basket. Set basket over 1″ boiling water in a saucepan. Cover saucepan with lid and let steam for about 5 to 8 minutes, or until broccoli is crisp yet tender. Remove broccoli and rinse in cold water; drain well. In a medium bowl, combine steamed broccoli, shredded Cheddar cheese, cubed ham, sliced green onions, parsley, nutmeg, salt and pepper. Toss together until well combined.

On a lightly floured flat surface, roll out pastry into 2 (8″ to 10″) circles. Place 1½ cups of the filling on 1 side of each pastry half; spread evenly and press down to flatten. In a small bowl, combine egg and heavy cream. Use a pastry brush to spread egg wash over pastry edges. Fold pastry over filling to make 4 turnovers. Use a fork to seal the edges and poke a few holes in the top of each pastry. Place the turnovers on a baking sheet and brush with remaining egg wash. Bake in oven for 18 to 22 minutes, or until pastry is golden brown. Remove from oven and let stand for 5 minutes before serving.

Makes 4 servings

Quick Chicken Quesadillas

Ingredients

1 C. shredded cooked chicken
½ C. shredded Cheddar cheese
½ C. chopped onion
½ C. shredded mozzarella cheese
2 (8″) flour tortillas
Ranch salad dressing

Directions

In a medium bowl, combine the shredded cooked chicken, shredded Cheddar cheese, chopped onion and shredded mozzarella cheese. Mix until well combined; set aside.

Spray nonstick cooking spray over 1 side of each tortilla. Place tortillas, greased side down, in a large skillet or on a preheated griddle. Spread chicken mixture over half of the tortilla. Fold over other side of tortilla to enclose the filling. Cook over low heat for 1 to 2 minutes, turning once, until both sides of tortilla are golden brown. Cut quesadillas into wedges and serve with ranch salad dressing for dipping.

Makes 2 servings

Ham 'n Swiss Stromboli

Ingredients

1 (11 oz.) pkg. refrigerated crusty French loaf dough
6 oz. thinly sliced deli ham
6 green onions, sliced
8 strips bacon, cooked and crumbled
1½ C. shredded Swiss cheese

Directions

Preheat oven to 350°. Unroll French loaf dough on a greased baking sheet. Spread sliced deli ham over dough to within ½″ of the edge. Sprinkle sliced green onions, crumbled bacon and shredded Swiss cheese over the ham; spread evenly. Roll up the dough, starting at the long side. Pinch the seams to seal and tuck the ends under. Position the roll so it is seam side down on the baking sheet.

Use a sharp knife to cut slits ¼″ deep into the top of the dough to allow steam to escape. Bake in oven for 26 to 30 minutes, or until dough is golden brown. Remove from oven and let cool for a few minutes before cutting into slices. Serve warm.

Makes 6 servings

Turkey Citrus Pitas

Ingredients

2 T. flour

½ tsp. pepper

1 T. plus 3 tsp. chilled unsalted butter or
  margarine, divided

2 tsp. olive oil

1 lb. turkey breast strips

1 C. pulp-free orange juice, divided

¼ C. orange marmalade

¼ tsp. dried sage or 1 tsp. fresh minced sage

2 pita bread rounds

Directions

On a shallow plate, combine flour and pepper. In a large
skillet over high heat, place 3 teaspoons butter and olive
oil. Dredge the turkey breast strips in flour, shaking off
any excess. Sauté coated turkey strips in skillet for 2 to
3 minutes per side, or until cooked throughout. Transfer
sautéed turkey strips to a platter and keep warm. Remove
grease from skillet and reduce heat to medium-high.

Add ½ cup orange juice to the skillet and bring to a boil
for 1 to 2 minutes, or until juice is reduced to a glaze. Add
remaining juice, marmalade and sage to the skillet. Boil
for an additional 2 minutes, or until sauce coats the back
of a spoon. Remove sauce from heat and stir in remaining
1 tablespoon butter and any juice from the turkey platter.

Cut each pita bread round in half to create 4 pockets. Stuff
an even amount of the turkey strips in each pocket. Pour
orange sauce over turkey and serve immediately.

Makes 4 servings

Beefy Mushroom Stuffed Pockets

Ingredients

1 (16 oz.) pkg. hot roll mix
1 lb. lean ground beef
1 (10¾ oz.) can cream of mushroom soup
1 (4 oz.) can mushroom pieces, drained
1 small onion, chopped
1 T. Worcestershire sauce
1 C. shredded Cheddar cheese
1 egg
2 T. water

Directions

Preheat oven to 400°. According to package directions, prepare hot roll mix for a pizza dough. While dough is rising, brown ground beef in a large skillet over high heat. Drain grease from skillet and stir in cream of mushroom soup, drained mushroom pieces, chopped onion and Worcestershire sauce. Heat for 1 to 2 minutes, stirring often, and remove from heat.

Divide the dough into 8 even pieces. Roll each dough piece into a ball. On a lightly floured flat surface, roll each ball into an 8″ circle. Place the dough circles on 2 lightly greased baking sheets. Divide the meat mixture evenly over the dough circles and sprinkle shredded Cheddar cheese over the meat.

In a small bowl, whisk together egg and water. Using a pastry brush, spread a little amount of the egg wash around the edge of the dough. Fold the dough over the filling and press down to enclose. Use a fork to press edges together. Brush the remaining egg wash over the dough. Bake in oven for 20 minutes. Remove from oven and let cool slightly before serving.

Makes 8 servings

Spinach-Walnut Pita Pockets

Ingredients

2 whole wheat pita bread rounds
¼ lb. watercress or lettuce leaves, washed
1 lb. spinach, washed
1 T. olive oil
½ C. finely chopped walnuts
1 tsp. dried rosemary or 2 tsp. fresh chopped rosemary
Salt and pepper to taste
¼ C. grated Parmesan cheese

Directions

Preheat oven to 200°. Wrap pita bread rounds in aluminum foil and place in oven to keep warm.

In a steamer basket over a saucepan with 1″ boiling water, place washed watercress. Steam for 30 seconds to 1 minute. Add washed spinach and steam for an additional 1 to 2 minutes, or until spinach just begins to wilt. Remove from heat and transfer watercress and spinach to a colander. Squeeze firmly to remove any excess moisture. Finely chop the watercress and spinach and set aside.

In a large skillet over medium heat, place olive oil. Once oil is hot, add finely chopped walnuts and rosemary and sauté for 1 minute. Stir in chopped watercress and spinach. Mix lightly and season with salt and pepper to taste. Remove from heat and stir in grated Parmesan cheese.

Remove pita rounds from oven and cut each round in half to make 4 pockets. Stuff an even amount of the spinach mixture in each pocket. Serve immediately.

Makes 4 servings

Thai Chicken Pitas

1 C. shredded cooked chicken
2 T. shredded mozzarella cheese
½ C. shredded carrots
2 T. chopped green onions
1 pita bread round
Thai peanut sauce

In a medium bowl, combined shredded cooked chicken, shredded mozzarella cheese, shredded carrots and chopped green onions. Toss all together until well combined.

Cut pita bread round in half, creating 2 pockets. Stuff an even amount of the chicken and carrot mixture into each pita pocket. Drizzle desired amount of Thai peanut sauce over ingredients in each pocket. Serve immediately.

Makes 2 servings

Cheddar Beef Turnover Bites

Ingredients

2 lbs. lean ground beef
1 small onion, chopped
1 (16 oz.) can refried beans
1 (8 oz.) can tomato sauce
2 tsp. chili powder
1 tsp. garlic powder
1 tsp. salt
½ tsp. pepper
½ tsp. paprika
Dash of cayenne pepper
2 (1 lb.) loaves frozen bread dough, thawed
1 C. shredded Cheddar cheese, divided

Directions

In a large skillet over medium heat, combine ground beef and chopped onion. Sauté until ground beef is browned and onion is softened. Add refried beans, tomato sauce, chili powder, garlic powder, salt, pepper, paprika and cayenne pepper. Bring mixture to a boil. Reduce heat, cover and let simmer for 15 minutes. Remove from heat and let cool.

Roll each loaf of dough into an 8 x 16″ rectangle, each about ¼″ thick. Cut each rectangle into 8 (4″) squares. Place about ¼ cup of the filling over each square. Sprinkle about 1 tablespoon shredded Cheddar cheese over filling. Fold the 4 corners of each square up and over the filling; pinch to seal. Place the turnover bites on greased baking sheets. Preheat oven to 350°. Cover baking sheets with towels and let rise for about 15 minutes. Bake in oven for 20 to 25 minutes, or until lightly browned. Remove from oven and serve immediately.

Makes 16 small servings

Sautéed Chicken Veggie Pitas

Ingredients

1 T. plus 1 tsp. olive oil, divided
2 red onions, sliced
2 red or green bell peppers, cut into long thin strips
Salt and pepper to taste
1 lb. boneless, skinless chicken breast halves,
    cut into ¼˝ strips
½ tsp. ground cumin
½ tsp. dried thyme or 2 tsp. fresh chopped thyme
1 (6 oz.) can sliced black olives, drained
2 pita bread rounds

Directions

In a large skillet over medium heat, place half of the olive oil. Once oil is hot, add sliced red onions, bell pepper strips, salt and pepper. Sauté for about 10 minutes, stirring often, until vegetables are very tender. Transfer sautéed vegetables to a platter and set aside.

Add remaining olive oil to skillet and increase heat to high. Sauté chicken strips in oil for 2 to 3 minutes, or until cooked throughout. Season with salt and pepper to taste. Return sautéed vegetables to skillet with chicken strips. Stir in ground cumin and thyme. Continue to cook until heated throughout. Remove from heat and stir in sliced black olives.

Cut each pita bread round in half, creating 4 pockets. Stuff an even amount of the mixture into each pita. Serve immediately.

Makes 4 servings

Pork Gyro Sandwiches

Ingredients

1 lb. boneless pork loin
¼ C. plus 1 T. olive oil
1 T. yellow mustard
½ C. lemon juice
2 cloves garlic, minced
1 tsp. dried oregano
1 C. plain lowfat yogurt
1 cucumber, peeled and chopped
½ tsp. crushed garlic
½ tsp. dried dillweed
2 pita bread rounds
1 small red onion, peeled and thinly sliced

Directions

Cut the pork loin crosswise into ½″ slices. Then cut each slice into 5″ strips. In a small bowl, combine olive oil, yellow mustard, lemon juice, minced garlic and dried oregano. Place pork slices in a shallow dish and pour marinade over, tossing lightly until evenly coated. Cover dish with plastic wrap and place in refrigerator to marinate for 1 to 8 hours.

In a separate bowl, combine yogurt, chopped cucumber, crushed garlic and dried dillweed. Cover bowl and place in refrigerator while pork is marinating.

Preheat oven to 450°. Drain marinade from pork slices and place pork in a single layer in a shallow pan. Roast pork in oven for about 10 minutes, or until crisp. Cut each pita bread round in half to create 4 pockets. Stuff an even amount of pork slices into each pita pocket. Drizzle some of the cucumber sauce over each pita and top with a few red onion slices before serving.

Makes 4 servings

Herb & Veggie Pita Pockets

Ingredients

1 T. plus 1 tsp. olive oil, divided
2 red onions, sliced
2 red or green bell peppers, cut into long thin strips
Salt and pepper to taste
1 lb. firm tofu, cut into 1″ strips
½ tsp. ground cumin
½ tsp. dried thyme or 2 tsp. fresh chopped thyme
1 (6 oz.) can sliced black olives, drained
2 pita bread rounds

Directions

In a large skillet over medium heat, place half of the olive oil. Once oil is hot, add sliced red onions, bell pepper strips, salt and pepper. Sauté for about 10 minutes, stirring often, until vegetables are very tender. Transfer sautéed vegetables to a platter and set aside.

Add remaining olive oil to skillet and increase to high heat. Sauté tofu in oil for 2 to 3 minutes, or until cooked throughout. Season with salt and pepper to taste. Return sautéed vegetables to skillet with tofu. Stir in ground cumin and thyme. Continue to cook until heated throughout. Remove from heat and stir in sliced black olives.

Cut each pita bread round in half, creating 4 pockets. Stuff an even amount of the mixture into each pita. Serve immediately.

Makes 4 servings

Beef & Cheddar Stuffed Sandwiches

Ingredients

1 loaf French bread, cut in half lengthwise
1 lb. lean ground beef
1 (10 ¾ oz.) can Cheddar cheese soup
1 medium green pepper, chopped
1 stalk celery, chopped
1 T. Worcestershire sauce
1 tsp. salt
½ tsp. pepper
4 slices American cheese, halved

Directions

Preheat oven to 350°. Scoop out bread from bottom half of French bread loaf to create a hollowed area for the filling. Tear removed bread into small pieces; set aside.

In a skillet over medium heat, brown ground beef. Drain grease from skillet and stir in Cheddar cheese soup, chopped green pepper, chopped celery, Worcestershire sauce, salt and pepper. Cook, stirring often, for 3 to 4 minutes. Stir in torn bread pieces. Stuff filling into hollowed bread half. Top with American cheese halves. Place top of loaf over cheese slices.

Place stuffed bread loaf on an ungreased baking sheet. Bake in oven for 6 to 8 minutes, or until cheese is melted. Remove from oven and cut into 8 equal portions. Serve immediately.

Makes 8 servings

Spinach Sausage Turnovers

Ingredients

½ lb. bulk pork sausage
⅓ C. chopped onion
1 clove garlic, minced
1 C. fresh chopped spinach
¼ C. fresh chopped mushrooms
¾ C. shredded mozzarella cheese
½ tsp. salt
¼ tsp. pepper
2 T. grated Parmesan cheese
2 (8 oz.) tubes crescent rolls
1 egg
1 T. water
1 T. cornmeal

Directions

Preheat oven to 350°. In a large skillet over high heat, sauté sausage, chopped onion and minced garlic. Drain grease from skillet. Remove skillet from heat and stir in chopped spinach, chopped mushrooms, shredded mozzarella cheese, salt, pepper and grated Parmesan cheese. Mix until well combined and set aside.

Unroll the tubes of crescent rolls. Form the 16 triangles into 8 equal rectangles, pinching the perforations together. Flatten each dough portion slightly into a 4½ x 5″ rectangle. Place about ⅓ cup of the sausage mixture over half of each rectangle. In a small bowl, whisk together egg and water. Use a pastry brush to spread egg wash over the inside edge of each rectangle. Bring dough up and over filling. Use a fork to seal the edge. Brush additional egg wash over the pastry.

Sprinkle cornmeal evenly over a greased baking sheet. Place turnovers on prepared baking sheet. Bake in oven for 15 to 20 minutes, or until crust is golden brown. Remove from oven and let cool slightly before serving.

Makes 8 servings

Shrimp Salad Pitas

2 C. cooked salad shrimp
3 kiwis, peeled, sliced and quartered
¾ C. shredded carrots
½ C. mayonnaise
½ C. chopped pecans
⅛ tsp. ground nutmeg
3 pita bread rounds
Lettuce leaves

In a medium bowl, combine cooked salad shrimp, quartered kiwis, shredded carrots, mayonnaise, chopped pecans and ground nutmeg. Mix until well combined.

Cut each pita bread round in half to create 6 pockets. Line the inside of each pocket with a few lettuce leaves. Stuff an even amount of the shrimp mixture in each pocket. Serve immediately.

Makes 6 servings

Stacked
Grilled, Filled & Panini

Deluxe Deli Panini

Ingredients

1 medium onion, sliced
1 C. fresh sliced mushrooms
1 C. julienned green pepper
1 C. julienned sweet red pepper
2 T. vegetable oil
¼ lb. thinly sliced deli honey ham
¼ lb. thinly sliced deli smoked turkey
¼ lb. thinly sliced deli pastrami
6 bacon strips, cooked and cut in half
12 slices sourdough bread
6 slices American cheese
6 slices Swiss cheese

Directions

In a large skillet over medium-high heat, sauté the sliced onion, sliced mushrooms, green pepper strips and sweet red pepper strips in vegetable oil. Heat, stirring often, until vegetables are tender.

Layer an even amount of the honey ham, smoked turkey, pastrami and bacon over 6 slices of bread. Divide the sautéed vegetables, American cheese and Swiss cheese over the meat on each sandwich. Top with remaining 6 bread slices.

Use a panini grill or panini press to grill sandwiches, 1 or 2 at a time, over medium-high heat. Cook until sandwiches are golden brown and cheese is melted. To serve, cut each sandwich in half diagonally.

Makes 6 servings

Honey-Mustard Chicken Sandwiches

Ingredients

¼ C. Dijon mustard
2 T. honey
1 tsp. dried oregano
1 tsp. water
¼ tsp. garlic powder
⅛ tsp. cayenne pepper
4 (4 oz.) boneless, skinless chicken breast halves
4 sandwich buns, split
8 thin slices tomato, divided
1 C. shredded lettuce, divided

Directions

Preheat broiler. In a medium bowl, combine Dijon mustard, honey, dried oregano, water, garlic powder and cayenne pepper; mix well. Place chicken breast halves on a broiler pan. Place pan under broiler so chicken is 4″ from the heat. Broil for 3 minutes on each side. Remove from broiler and brush a generous amount of the mustard mixture over chicken. Return to broiler for an additional 4 to 6 minutes, or until juices run clear and chicken is cooked throughout.

Place 1 chicken breast half on each sandwich bun. Place 2 tomato slices and some of the shredded lettuce over chicken on each sandwich; top with buns tops and serve immediately.

Makes 4 servings

Hawaiian Chicken Sandwiches

Ingredients

1 (20 oz.) can sliced pineapple
1 T. brown sugar
1 tsp. ground mustard
1 tsp. garlic salt
½ tsp. pepper
6 boneless, skinless chicken breast halves
¼ C. mayonnaise
1 T. Dijon mustard
¼ tsp. dried dillweed
6 kaiser rolls, split and toasted
6 lettuce leaves

Directions

Drain liquid from pineapple, reserving 1 cup of the juice and 6 pineapple slices. Set aside remaining juice and pineapple slices for another use. In a large resealable bag, combine brown sugar, ground mustard, garlic salt and pepper. Add the 1 cup reserved pineapple juice. Add chicken breast halves to bag, turning to coat. Refrigerate for at least 2 hours, turning bag occasionally. In a small bowl, combine mayonnaise, Dijon mustard and dried dillweed. Refrigerate until ready to use.

Remove chicken from refrigerator and discard the marinade. Grill chicken over medium heat for 5 to 6 minutes per side, or until juices run clear and chicken is cooked throughout. Grill the 6 pineapple slices for 1 minute on each side. Spread mayonnaise mixture over toasted rolls. Place 1 lettuce leaf on each roll and assemble each sandwich with 1 grilled chicken breast half and 1 grilled pineapple slice. Serve immediately.

Makes 6 servings

Grilled Garden Panini

Ingredients

2 T. mayonnaise
4 slices sourdough bread
1 C. shredded Cheddar cheese
2 small zucchinis, halved lengthwise
1 large tomato, thinly sliced
¼ C. shredded carrots
1 T. shelled and salted sunflower seeds
2 T. butter or margarine, softened

Directions

Spread mayonnaise over 1 side of each bread slice. On 2 of the slices, layer the shredded Cheddar cheese, zucchini slices, sliced tomato, shredded carrots and sunflower seeds. Top with remaining 2 bread slices, mayonnaise side down. Spread butter over outer sides of the sandwich bread.

Use a panini grill or panini press to grill sandwiches over medium-high heat. Cook until sandwich is golden brown and cheese is melted. To serve, cut each sandwich in half diagonally.

Makes 2 servings

BBQ Grilled Chicken Sandwiches

Ingredients

1½ lbs. boneless, skinless chicken breast halves
½ C. barbecue sauce
1 C. mayonnaise
½ C. finely chopped onion
½ C. chopped celery
¼ tsp. salt
¼ tsp. crushed red pepper flakes
8 kaiser rolls, split
8 tomato slices
8 lettuce leaves

Directions

Place chicken breast halves in a large resealable plastic bag. Add barbecue sauce, seal bag and turn gently to coat the chicken. Let chicken marinate in refrigerator overnight or at least 8 hours.

Preheat grill to medium-high heat. Place chicken on grill, cover and cook for 6 to 8 minutes per side, or until juices run clear. Remove from grill and let cool. Place chicken in refrigerator until chilled. Once chilled, chop chicken into small pieces and place in a medium bowl. Add mayonnaise, chopped onion, chopped celery, salt and red pepper flakes. Toss together until well blended. Spoon an even amount of the chicken salad over each roll. Top each serving with 1 tomato slice and 1 lettuce leaf. Serve immediately or place in refrigerator until ready to serve.

Makes 8 servings

Grilled Chicken Apple Sandwiches

1 (12 oz.) can chunked chicken, drained
$\frac{1}{3}$ C. mayonnaise
1½ C. shredded Swiss cheese
1 to 2 tsp. lemon juice
2 stalks celery, chopped
1 apple, finely chopped
12 slices whole wheat bread
2 T. butter, softened

Directions

In a small bowl, combine chunked chicken, mayonnaise, shredded Swiss cheese, lemon juice, chopped celery and finely chopped apple. Mix until well blended.

Spread 1 side of each bread slice with butter. Divide chicken and apple mixture evenly over half of the bread slices and top with remaining bread slices, buttered side out. Grill sandwiches in a large skillet over medium heat, turning once, until cheese begins to melt and bread is toasted.

Makes 6 servings

Chicken Cordon Bleu Panino

Ingredients

2 T. butter, softened
2 slices whole wheat bread
1 T. sour cream
2 slices Swiss cheese
1 thick slice cooked chicken breast meat
1 slice deli ham

Directions

Spread butter over 1 side of each bread slice. Spread sour cream over the other side of each bread slice.

To assemble sandwich, layer 1 Swiss cheese slice over sour cream side of 1 bread slice. Top with chicken breast slice, deli ham slice, remaining Swiss cheese slice and remaining bread slice, sour cream side down.

To make a panino sandwich, use a panini grill or panini press to grill sandwich over medium-high heat. Cook until sandwich is golden brown and cheese is melted. To serve, cut sandwich in half diagonally. To make a grilled sandwich, in a small skillet over medium heat, grill sandwich, turning once, until bread is lightly browned and cheese is melted.

Makes 1 serving

Caesar Chicken Salad Sandwiches

Ingredients

2 boneless, skinless chicken breast halves
3 tsp. lemon juice, divided
2 tsp. soy sauce
3 T. mayonnaise
2 T. grated Parmesan cheese
1 tsp. Dijon mustard
½ tsp. anchovy paste
½ tsp. minced garlic
⅛ tsp. pepper
4 slices whole grain bread
2 lettuce leaves
4 slices tomato

Directions

Preheat broiler. In a large resealable plastic bag, place chicken breast halves. Add 2 teaspoons lemon juice and soy sauce to bag, seal and let marinate in refrigerator for 10 minutes. Remove chicken from bag and place on a broiler pan. Place pan under broiler so chicken is 5″ to 6″ from the heat. Broil chicken for 6 minutes on each side, or until juices run clear and chicken is cooked throughout. Remove chicken from broiler and let cool. Once cooled, chop or shred chicken into small pieces.

In a medium bowl, combine shredded chicken, remaining 2 teaspoons lemon juice, mayonnaise, grated Parmesan cheese, Dijon mustard, anchovy paste, minced garlic and pepper. Toss all together until well combined. Spread about 1 cup of the chicken salad over 2 slices of bread. Place 1 lettuce leaf and 2 tomato slices over chicken salad. Top with remaining bread slices. Serve immediately or place in refrigerator until ready to serve.

Makes 2 servings

Tangy Turkey Sandwiches

Ingredients

½ C. chopped green pepper
⅓ C. chopped onion
2 T. butter
1½ C. ketchup
½ C. chicken broth
1½ tsp. Worcestershire sauce
1 tsp. yellow mustard
¼ tsp. hot pepper sauce
¼ tsp. pepper
3 C. cooked cubed turkey
4 sandwich buns, split

Directions

In a large saucepan over medium-high heat, sauté chopped green pepper and chopped onion in butter until softened. Stir in ketchup, chicken broth, Worcestershire sauce, yellow mustard, hot pepper sauce and pepper. Mix in cubed turkey. Remove from heat and simmer, uncovered, for about 20 minutes, or until heated throughout. To assemble sandwiches, use a slotted spoon to pile turkey mixture onto sandwich buns.

Makes 4 servings

Sourdough Panino Ham & Cheese

2 tsp. mayonnaise
2 slices sourdough bread
2 slices Provolone cheese
2 thin slices deli ham
½ roasted red pepper, sliced
2 tsp. butter, softened
2 tsp. grated Parmesan or Romano cheese

Directions

Spread mayonnaise over 1 side of each slice of bread. On 1 of the slices, layer the Provolone cheese, deli ham and sliced red pepper. Top with remaining slice of bread, mayonnaise side down. Spread butter over outer sides of the sandwich bread. Sprinkle grated Parmesan cheese over the buttered side of the sandwich.

Use a panini grill or panini press to grill sandwich over medium-high heat. Cook until sandwich is golden brown and cheese is melted. To serve, cut sandwich in half diagonally.

Makes 1 serving

Zesty Pork Sandwiches

Ingredients

¼ C. butter or margarine
¼ C. Worcestershire sauce
2 T. lemon juice
2 T. sugar
¼ tsp. paprika
⅛ tsp. salt
⅛ tsp. cayenne pepper
½ lb. thinly sliced cooked pork
2 to 4 sandwich buns, split

Directions

In a large saucepan over medium heat, combine butter, Worcestershire sauce, lemon juice, sugar, paprika, salt and cayenne pepper. Bring mixture to a boil, stirring frequently. Add sliced pork and simmer until heated throughout, stirring often. Divide meat mixture evenly over sandwich buns. Drizzle 1 tablespoon sauce over the meat on each sandwich. Serve sandwiches with remaining sauce on the side.

Makes 2 to 4 servings

Ham & Bell Pepper Hoagies

Ingredients

1 T. olive oil
1 green bell pepper, sliced into rings
1 clove garlic, minced
½ tsp. dried onion flakes
½ lb. thinly sliced cooked ham
1 medium tomato, sliced
2 to 4 hoagie sandwich buns, split
½ tsp. dried oregano
¼ lb. thinly sliced Provolone cheese

Directions

Preheat oven to 350°. In a large skillet over medium heat, place olive oil. Add green bell pepper rings and minced garlic. Sauté until vegetables are tender. Add dried onion flakes and toss until well combined. Remove sautéed mixture from skillet, reserving oil mixture in skillet.

Divide ham, sliced tomato and sautéed mixture onto bottom half of hoagie buns. Drizzle reserved oil mixture over ingredients and sprinkle with oregano. Top with Provolone cheese slices and top half of each bun. Wrap each sandwich in aluminum foil and place in oven. Bake for 25 minutes. Remove sandwiches from oven, unwrap and cut each hoagie in half. Serve immediately.

Makes 2 to 4 servings

Chicken Fiesta Panini

Ingredients

7 green olives, pitted
1 small clove garlic, peeled
2 T. drained capers
Zest of 1 lemon
3 T. olive oil
4 T. lemon juice
Pinch of salt and pepper
8 slices sourdough bread or 4 sandwich rolls
2 boneless, skinless chicken breast halves,
    roasted and thinly sliced

Directions

In a food processor, combine green olives, peeled garlic clove, capers and zest of 1 lemon. Process until well combined. Transfer mixture to a bowl. In a small jar with a tight-fitting lid, combine olive oil and lemon juice. Shake until well combined and pour over ingredients in bowl. Stir in salt and pepper. Cover bowl and refrigerate until ready to serve.

Over 4 slices of bread or over the bottom half of each roll, spread an even amount of the olive mixture leaving some of the juices in the bowl. Place a few slices of chicken over the olive mixture on each sandwich. Top with bun tops or remaining slices of bread. Use a pastry brush to spread the remaining juices over sandwiches and press down lightly.

Use a panini grill or panini press to grill sandwiches over medium-high heat. Cook until sandwiches are golden brown and heated throughout. To serve, cut each sandwich in half diagonally.

Makes 4 servings

Creamy Tuna & Veggie Sandwiches

Ingredients

1 (6 oz.) can tuna, drained
⅔ C. chopped cucumber
½ C. shredded carrots
¼ C. finely chopped green onions
¼ C. mayonnaise
¼ C. Dijon mustard
2 T. sour cream
1 T. lemon juice
Pepper to taste
8 slices whole wheat bread
4 lettuce leaves

Directions

In a medium bowl, combine drained tuna, chopped cucumber, shredded carrots, chopped green onions, mayonnaise, Dijon mustard, sour cream, lemon juice and pepper. Mix until well combined.

Divide the mixture evenly onto 4 of the bread slices. Place 1 lettuce leaf on each sandwich. Top with remaining 4 bread slices. Serve immediately.

Makes 4 servings

Panini with Proscuitto & Provolone

Ingredients

2 T. butter, melted
4 boneless, skinless chicken breast halves
2 tsp. fresh chopped sage or ½ tsp. dried sage
2 tsp. fresh chopped rosemary or ½ tsp. dried rosemary
Salt and pepper to taste
4 crusty rolls (French, Italian or sourdough)
⅓ C. balsamic vinaigrette dressing
2 C. arugula, washed and dried
8 slices proscuitto
8 slices Provolone

Directions

Preheat broiler or grill to medium-high heat. Use a pastry brush to spread melted butter over chicken breast halves. In a small bowl, combine sage and rosemary; sprinkle over chicken. Season chicken with salt and pepper to taste. Grill chicken until cooked throughout or place under broiler until juices run clear and chicken is no longer pink on the inside.

Slice each roll in half diagonally. Spread some of the vinaigrette over the bottom of each roll and top with some of the arugula. Layer 2 slices proscuitto and 2 slices Provolone over each roll. Cut each cooked chicken breast half into ½″ thick diagonal slices. Place over Provolone on each roll. Drizzle more vinaigrette over chicken slices and place top half of each roll over top. Press down gently on each sandwich.

Use a panini grill or panini press to grill sandwiches over medium-high heat. Cook until sandwiches are golden brown and heated throughout. To serve, cut each sandwich in half diagonally.

Makes 4 servings

Grilled Fish Sandwiches

Ingredients

4 (4 oz.) cod fillets
1 T. lime juice
½ tsp. lemon-pepper seasoning
¼ C. mayonnaise
2 tsp. Dijon mustard
1 tsp. honey
4 sandwich buns, split
4 lettuce leaves
4 tomato slices

Directions

Brush both sides of each fillet with lime juice. Sprinkle lemon-pepper seasoning over each fillet. Preheat grill to medium heat and coat the grill rack with nonstick cooking spray. Place seasoned fillets on rack and heat for 5 to 6 minutes on each side, or until fish flakes easily with a fork.

In a small bowl, combine mayonnaise, Dijon mustard and honey. Spread mixture over the bottom of each bun. Place 1 grilled fillet on each bun. Place 1 lettuce leaf and 1 tomato slice over fillet and top with bun tops. Serve immediately.

Makes 4 servings

Quick Seafood Subs

Ingredients

5 oz. lump crabmeat or imitation crabmeat, flaked
¾ C. mayonnaise
2 stalks celery, chopped
3 T. finely chopped green onions
4 hoagie sandwich buns, split
4 lettuce leaves

Directions

In a medium bowl, combine crabmeat, mayonnaise, chopped celery and finely chopped green onions. Mix until well combined.

Divide mixture evenly over hoagie buns. Place 1 lettuce leaf on each sandwich. Serve immediately.

Makes 4 servings

Apple & Brie Stuffed Panini

Ingredients

12 slices bacon
3 T. butter, divided
1 large Golden Delicious apple, cored and thinly sliced
Dijon mustard
1(1 lb.) loaf focaccia bread
1 (16 oz.) round Brie cheese, rind trimmed,
  cut into 16 slices

Directions

In a large skillet over medium heat, cook bacon until crisp. Transfer bacon to paper towels to drain and wipe skillet clean.

Add 1 tablespoon butter to same skillet. Once the butter is melted, add apples slices to skillet and sauté for about 4 minutes. Remove from heat.

Cut focaccia loaf crosswise into 4 pieces. Then cut each piece in half horizontally. Spread Dijon mustard over the inside of all bread pieces. Place 2 Brie cheese slices on the bottom half of the 4 bread pieces. Top each with an even amount of the sautéed apple slices. Place 3 cooked bacon slices on each and top with remaining Brie cheese slices. Press down gently on each sandwich.

Use a panini grill or panini press to grill sandwiches over medium-high heat. Cook until sandwiches are golden brown and heated throughout. To serve, cut each sandwich in half diagonally.

Makes 4 servings

Deluxe Grilled Cheese Sandwiches

Ingredients

1 (3 oz.) pkg. cream cheese, softened
¾ C. mayonnaise
1 C. shredded Colby-Monterey Jack cheese blend
¾ tsp. garlic salt
8 slices bread
2 T. butter, softened

Directions

In a medium bowl, combine cream cheese, mayonnaise, shredded cheese and garlic salt. Mix until well blended.

Preheat a large skillet over medium heat. Spread the cheese mixture over 4 slices of bread; top with remaining 4 bread slices. Spread butter over outer sides of the sandwich bread.

Grill sandwiches in preheated skillet, turning once, until sandwiches are golden brown and heated throughout. To serve, cut each sandwich in half diagonally.

Makes 4 servings

Mediterranean Veggie Sandwiches

Ingredients

1 eggplant, sliced into strips
2 red bell peppers
2 T. olive oil, divided
2 Portobello mushrooms, sliced
1 (1 lb.) loaf focaccia bread
3 cloves garlic, crushed
4 T. mayonnaise

Directions

Preheat oven to 400°. Place eggplant strips and whole red bell peppers on a baking sheet. Use a pastry brush to spread 1 tablespoon olive oil over the eggplant strips and red bell peppers. Place baking sheet in oven and roast vegetables. The eggplant should be tender after 25 minutes. Roast the red pepper until the outer skin is blackened. Once roasted, remove vegetables from oven and let cool.

In a small skillet over medium heat, sauté sliced Portobello mushrooms in remaining olive oil. Slice the focaccia bread in half lengthwise. In a small bowl, combine crushed garlic and mayonnaise. Spread mayonnaise mixture over both sides of bread.

Remove the blackened skin from the red pepper, core and slice. Arrange roasted eggplant strips, sliced peppers and sautéed mushrooms over the focaccia bread. Place top half of bread over vegetables. Cut sandwich into slices and serve immediately. If a flattened focaccia sandwich is preferred, wrap sandwich in plastic wrap. Place a cutting board over the sandwich and set canned foods on the cutting board to flatten the sandwich. Allow sandwich to flatten for 1 to 2 hours before removing the plastic wrap and slicing into 6 servings.

Makes 6 servings

Artichoke Tuna Panini

Ingredients

4 large crusty rolls
2 (6 oz.) cans tuna
8 canned artichoke hearts, drained
4 T. canned roasted red peppers,
    drained and chopped, divided
4 tsp. chopped black olives, divided
4 T. fresh chopped basil, divided
4 tsp. olive oil, divided
Pepper to taste
Juice of 1 lemon

Directions

Cut each roll in half horizontally. Remove some of the bread to form a pocket in each roll.

Drain the tuna and cut each artichoke heart into quarters. Over the bottom half of each roll, layer an even amount of the tuna, artichoke quarters, chopped roasted peppers, chopped olives and chopped basil. Drizzle 1 teaspoon olive oil over each sandwich and season with pepper to taste. Sprinkle lemon juice over ingredients on each sandwich and replace tops of rolls.

Use a panini grill or panini press to grill sandwiches over medium-high heat. Cook until sandwiches are golden brown and heated throughout. To serve, cut each sandwich in half diagonally.

Makes 4 servings

Grilled Havarti Sourdough Sandwiches

Ingredients

1½ C. cole slaw mix
½ C. bean sprouts
3 T. butter, softened
8 (¾″ thick) slices sourdough bread
3 T. honey mustard
6 oz. sliced Havarti cheese

Directions

In a medium bowl, toss together cole slaw mix and bean sprouts. Spread butter over 1 side of each bread slice. Spread honey mustard over the other side of 4 of the bread slices. Layer the cole slaw mixture over the honey mustard side of 4 slices. Divide Havarti cheese slices over cole slaw mixture and top with remaining 4 bread slices, buttered side out.

In a medium skillet over medium heat, grill sandwiches. Heat, turning once, until sandwiches are golden brown and heated throughout. To serve, cut each sandwich in half diagonally.

Makes 4 servings

Veggie Lovers Panini

Ingredients

¼ C. mayonnaise
3 cloves garlic, minced
1 T. lemon juice
⅛ C. olive oil
1 C. sliced red bell peppers
1 small zucchini, sliced
1 red onion, sliced
1 small yellow squash, sliced
2 (4x6″) focaccia bread pieces, split
½ C. crumbled feta cheese

Directions

In a small bowl, combine mayonnaise, minced garlic and lemon juice. Mix well and set aside in refrigerator. Preheat grill to high heat and lightly oil the grate.

Using a pastry brush, brush olive oil over sliced red bell peppers, sliced zucchini, sliced red onion and sliced yellow squash. Place red bell pepper slices and zucchini slices in the center of the grill. Place onion slices and yellow squash slices around red bell pepper. Cook for about 3 minutes, turn and cook for an additional 3 minutes. The peppers may take a little longer. Once softened, remove vegetables from grill and set aside.

Spread some of the mayonnaise mixture on the inside of each foccacia bread slice. Sprinkle some of the crumbled feta cheese over the buttered side of each bread slice and place, cheese side up, on the grill for 2 to 3 minutes. Remove bread from grill and assemble sandwiches by dividing roasted vegetables evenly between the foccaccia bread.

Use a panini grill or panini press to grill sandwiches over medium-high heat. Cook until sandwiches are golden brown and heated throughout. To serve, cut each sandwich in half diagonally.

Makes 2 servings

Shredded Barbecue Beef Sandwiches

Ingredients

3 lbs. beef stew meat, cut into 1″ cubes
3 medium green bell peppers, diced
2 large onions, diced
1 (6 oz.) can tomato paste
½ C. brown sugar
¼ C. cider vinegar
3 T. chili powder
2 tsp. salt
2 tsp. Worcestershire sauce
1 tsp. ground mustard
14 sandwich buns, split

Directions

In a 6-quart slow cooker, combine the beef stew meat, diced green bell peppers and diced onions. In a small bowl, mix together the tomato paste, brown sugar, cider vinegar, chili powder, salt, Worcestershire sauce and ground mustard. Stir tomato paste into meat mixture in slow cooker. Cover and cook on high for 7 to 8 hours, or until meat is tender.

Remove beef cubes from slow cooker and let cool slightly. Skim any grease from the liquid remaining in the slow cooker. Use 2 forks to shred beef into small pieces. Return shredded beef to the slow cooker. To serve, use a slotted spoon to pile about ½ cup of the beef mixture onto each sandwich bun.

Makes 14 servings

Crab Cake Panini

Ingredients

2 cloves garlic
½ C. fresh basil leaves
6 T. olive oil, divided
2 T. grated Parmesan cheese
¾ C. mayonnaise
Salt and pepper to taste
½ C. chopped red onion
½ T. red wine vinegar
½ tsp. fresh minced oregano
⅓ C. plus ¼ C. minced green onions, divided
⅓ C. minced celery
½ C. cracker crumbs
1 egg
2 T. fresh minced parsley
1½ tsp. seafood seasoning
½ tsp. salt
1 lb. lump crab meat, flaked
8 crusty rolls or 16 slices sourdough bread

Directions

In a food processor, combine garlic cloves, basil leaves, 3 tablespoons olive oil, grated Parmesan cheese, mayonnaise, salt and pepper. Process into a paste; set aside.

In a small bowl, combine chopped red onion, red wine vinegar and minced oregano; set aside.

Preheat broiler. In a frying pan over medium-high heat, heat remaining 3 tablespoons olive oil. Sauté ⅓ cup green onions and celery until softened.

In a large bowl, combine cracker crumbs, remaining ¼ cup green onions, egg, minced parsley, seafood seasoning and ½ teaspoon salt. Add the sautéed green onions and celery. Gently mix in the lump crab meat until well combined. Form mixture into 8 small cakes. Place cakes on a baking sheet and place under broiler for about 4 minutes. Gently turn over crab cakes and return to broiler for an additional 4 minutes, or until cakes are nicely browned.

Slice each roll in half horizontally. Brush the outside of each roll with additional olive oil. Divide basil paste evenly over bottom half of each roll. Place 1 crab cake on each and top with an even amount of the red onion relish. Place the top on each roll and press down gently.

Use a panini grill or panini press to grill sandwiches over medium-high heat. Cook until sandwiches are golden brown and heated throughout. To serve, cut each sandwich in half diagonally.

Makes 8 servings

Easy Italian Beef Hoagies

Ingredients

1 (4 lb.) boneless sirloin tip roast, halved
2 (¾ oz.) pkgs. Italian dressing mix
2 C. water
1 (16 oz.) jar mild jalapeno pepper slices
18 hoagie sandwich buns, split

Directions

In a 6-quart slow cooker, place roast halves. In a small bowl, combine Italian dressing mix and water; pour over roast in slow cooker. Cover and cook on low for 8 hours, or until meat is tender.

Remove roast meat from slow cooker and let cool slightly. Skim any grease from the liquid remaining in the slow cooker. Use 2 forks to shred beef into small pieces. Return shredded beef to the slow cooker. Stir in desired amount of jalapeno pepper slices. To serve, use a slotted spoon to pile about ½ cup of the beef and pepper mixture onto each sandwich bun.

Makes 18 servings

Horseradish Beef Steak Sandwiches

Ingredients

1 tsp. seasoned salt
½ to 1 tsp. pepper
1 (2″ thick) chuck or round steak, tenderized
½ C. unsalted butter, softened
2 T. yellow mustard
1 T. prepared horseradish
1 French bread loaf, split

Directions

Preheat grill to medium-high heat. Sprinkle seasoned salt and pepper over both sides of steak. Cook grill on the steak to desired doneness, turning frequently.

In a small bowl, combine butter, mustard and horseradish; mix well. Transfer cooked steak to a platter, cover and let stand for 5 to 10 minutes. Slice meat diagonally into very thin slices. Meanwhile, toast both sides of bread loaf over the grill for 1 to 2 minutes. Spread butter mixture over the grilled side of the bread. Layer thin steak slices over the bottom half of the loaf; drizzle juices from the platter over top. Season with additional pepper to taste and top with remaining bread half. Cut into 8 equal portions and serve immediately.

Makes 8 servings

Italian Grilled Steak Sandwiches

4 beef cube or minute steaks
1 pkg. dry onion soup mix
½ C. water
4 crusty Italian rolls, split
1 C. shredded Cheddar cheese
Salt and pepper to taste

Directions

In a large skillet over medium-high heat, cook steaks for 2 to 3 minutes, turning once. Remove steaks from skillet and set on a platter. Add dry onion soup mix to the skillet and cook for 2 to 3 minutes. Return steaks to skillet and heat for an additional 1 to 2 minutes, or until steaks are cooked to desired doneness.

Place 1 cooked steak on each Italian roll. Sprinkle some of the shredded Cheddar cheese over each steak and top with some of the onion mixture from the skillet; season with salt and pepper to taste. Serve immediately.

Makes 4 servings

Mozzarella & Tomato Panini

8 slices mozzarella cheese
8 slices sourdough or thin-sliced Italian bread
½ C. pesto sauce
1 large tomato, sliced
2 T. olive oil

Directions

Preheat grill to medium heat. Place 2 slices mozzarella cheese over 4 of the bread slices. Spread an even amount of the pesto sauce over cheese on each sandwich and top with a few tomato slices. Place remaining 4 slices of bread over tomato slices. Use a pastry brush to spread olive oil over the outer sides of the sandwich bread.

Use a panini grill or panini press to grill sandwiches over medium-high heat. Cook until sandwich is golden brown and cheese is melted. To serve, cut each sandwich in half diagonally.

Makes 4 servings

Juicy Sirloin Sandwiches

Ingredients

1 C. soy sauce
½ C. vegetable oil
½ C. cranberry or apple juice
1 (3 lb.) boneless beef sirloin tip roast
1 (1 oz.) pkg. au jus gravy mix
12 French rolls, split

Directions

In a large resealable plastic bag or shallow glass dish, combine soy sauce, vegetable oil and cranberry juice; mix well. Set aside ½ cup of the liquid marinade in the refrigerator for basting. Add the roast to the remaining marinade in the bag or dish, turning to coat. Seal bag or cover dish and place in refrigerator for 8 hours or overnight, turning once or twice.

Remove roast from refrigerator and discard the marinade. Preheat grill to medium heat. Cook the roast over indirect heat, basting and turning every 15 minutes. Grill roast for about 1 hour, or until meat reaches desired doneness. A meat thermometer should read 145° for medium-rare, 160° for medium, and 170° for well-done. Remove roast from grill and let cool to room temperature. Cover roast and refrigerate overnight.

In a large saucepan, prepare au jus mix according to package directions. Cut the roast into very thin slices. Add meat slices to the au jus mixture and cook until heated throughout. To serve, use a slotted spoon to pile roast. If desired, serve with au jus on the side for dipping.

Makes 12 servings

Zesty Barbecue Sandwich Bites

Ingredients

1 (10 oz.) tube refrigerated buttermilk biscuits
1 lb. lean ground beef
½ C. ketchup
3 T. brown sugar
1 T. cider vinegar
½ tsp. chili powder
1 C. shredded Cheddar cheese, divided

Directions

Preheat oven to 375°. Separate dough into 10 biscuits. Flatten each biscuit into a 5″ circle. In a greased muffin tin, press each dough circle into the bottom and up sides of 1 muffin cup; set aside.

In a large skillet over medium-high heat, cook ground beef until evenly browned. Drain grease from skillet. In a small bowl, combine ketchup, brown sugar, cider vinegar and chili powder; mix until smooth. Add ketchup mixture to ground beef and mix well. Divide meat mixture evenly into each biscuit-lined muffin cup. Sprinkle a little shredded Cheddar cheese over each serving. Bake in oven for 18 to 20 minutes, or until biscuits are golden brown. Remove from oven and let cool for about 5 minutes. Carefully remove muffins from tins and serve immediately.

Makes 10 servings

Reuben Panini

¾ C. thousand island dressing
8 slices rye bread
1 (16 oz.) can sauerkraut, drained
4 slices Swiss cheese
8 slices pastrami
¼ C. margarine, softened

Spread thousand island dressing over 1 side of each slice of rye bread. Over the dressing side of 4 of the bread slices, spread an even layer of sauerkraut. Top each sandwich with 1 Swiss cheese slice and 2 slices of pastrami. Top with remaining 4 bread slices, dressing side down. Spread butter over outer sides of the sandwich bread.

Use a panini grill or panini press to grill sandwiches over medium-high heat. Cook until sandwiches are golden brown and heated throughout. To serve, cut each sandwich in half diagonally.

Makes 4 servings

Dessert
Ice Cream, Cookies & Chocolate

Family Favorite Ice Cream Sandwiches

Ingredients

4 scoops ice cream or frozen yogurt, any kind
8 large cookies, any kind
4 T. miniature chocolate chips or chocolate sprinkles

Directions

Allow ice cream or frozen yogurt to soften slightly. Spread 1 scoop of softened ice cream over 4 of the cookies. Top with remaining 4 cookies to create sandwiches.

Place miniature chocolate chips or chocolate sprinkles in a shallow baking dish. Roll the ice cream edge of the cookies in baking dish until coated with chocolate chips. Wrap each sandwich in waxed paper and place in freezer at least 2 hours before serving.

Makes 4 servings

Happy Trails Ice Cream Waffle Sandwich

Ingredients

2 frozen waffles
1 T. chopped nuts
1 slice vanilla ice cream, slightly softened
1 T. chopped dried mixed fruits

Directions

Toast the 2 frozen waffles in the toaster. Place toasted waffles on a plate. Sprinkle chopped nuts over 1 of the waffles.

Cut 1 slice, about ½″ to ¾″ thick, from a block of ice cream. Place ice cream slice over the chopped nuts on the waffle. Sprinkle the dried mixed fruits over the slice of ice cream. Top with remaining waffle to create a sandwich. Wrap sandwich in waxed paper and place in freezer at least 2 hours before serving.

Makes 1 serving

Chocolate Peanut Butter
Ice Cream Sandwiches

Ingredients

30 peanut butter cookies
1 pt. chocolate ice cream, slightly softened
1 (6 oz.) pkg. chocolate chips
2 T. shortening

Directions

Place 15 of the cookies, flat side up, on the counter. Spread 1 rounded tablespoon of ice cream over the cookies and top with remaining 15 cookies to create sandwiches. Place cookie sandwiches on a jellyroll pan and place in freezer until firm, at least 2 hours.

In a double boiler over boiling water, place chocolate chips and shortening. Heat, stirring often, until chocolate is completely melted. Let stand for 2 minutes. Dip each sandwich into the melted chocolate. Cover the sandwiches completely or, if desired, only dip half in the chocolate. Return sandwiches to jellyroll pan and place in freezer until firm. Once firm, wrap each sandwich in plastic wrap and store in freezer until ready to serve.

Makes 15 servings

Hawaiian Ice Cream Sandwiches

Ingredients

24 (3″) chewy chocolate chip cookies
1 qt. chocolate chip ice cream, slightly softened
½ C. shredded coconut
1 medium banana, chopped

Directions

Bake or purchase any kind of chewy chocolate chip cookies. In a large bowl, combine softened chocolate ice cream, shredded coconut and chopped banana until well blended. Place mixture in freezer for about 2 hours.

Remove ice cream mixture from freezer and soften slightly. Spread about ¼ cup of the ice cream mixture over 12 of the cookies. Top each with an additional cookie, pressing together to form 12 sandwiches. Use a knife or spatula to quickly run around the edge of each sandwich, removing any excess ice cream. Wrap each sandwich in plastic wrap and place in freezer at least 4 hours before serving.

Makes 12 servings

Peppermint Chocolate
Ice Cream Sandwiches

Ingredients

1 pt. vanilla ice cream, slightly softened
¼ tsp. peppermint extract
¼ lb. (1 C.) finely crushed peppermint candies, divided
16 large chocolate wafers

Directions

In a large bowl, combine softened vanilla ice cream, peppermint extract and ½ cup finely crushed peppermint candies until well blended. Place mixture in freezer for about 2 hours.

Spread about ¼ cup of the ice cream mixture over each of the 8 chocolate wafers. Top each with an additional wafer, pressing together to form 8 sandwiches. Use a knife or spatula to quickly run around the edge of each sandwich, removing any excess ice cream. Place cookie sandwiches on a jellyroll pan and place in freezer for 1 hour. Spread remaining ½ cup crushed peppermint candies in a shallow dish. Roll the ice cream edge of the cookies in baking dish until coated with peppermint candies. Wrap each sandwich in plastic wrap and place in freezer at least 4 hours before serving.

Makes 8 servings

Devil's Food Ice Cream Sandwiches

Ingredients

1 egg
½ C. shortening
¼ C. butter, softened
1 tsp. vanilla
1 (17 ¾ oz.) pkg. devil's food cake mix, divided
½ gal. ice cream, slightly softened

Directions

Preheat oven to 375°. In a medium bowl, beat together egg, shortening, butter, vanilla and half of the dry cake mix. Mix until smooth. Stir in remaining cake mix and stir until a dough is formed. Divide dough into 4 equal parts. Roll each part into a 6 x 10″ rectangle. Cut each rectangle into 8 (2½ x 3″) smaller rectangles. Place rectangles on a parchment-lined baking sheet and prick lightly with a fork. Bake in oven until crisp, about 5 to 10 minutes. Remove from oven and let cool.

To assemble sandwiches, spread 1 to 2 tablespoons of the softened ice cream over half of the cookies; top with remaining cookies. Wrap each sandwich in plastic wrap and place in freezer at least 4 hours before serving.

Makes about 16 servings

Peanut Butter Banana Roll-Ups

Ingredients

4 (10″) flour tortillas
4 T. chunky peanut butter
4 bananas, lightly mashed
¼ C. honey
½ tsp. cinnamon

Directions

Lay tortillas on a flat surface. Spread 1 tablespoon peanut butter over each tortilla. Spread ¼ of the mashed bananas over peanut butter on each tortilla. Drizzle honey over banana and sprinkle with cinnamon.

Roll up the tortillas, folding the ends under to seal like a burrito. Preheat grill to medium heat. Place the rolled tortillas on grill for about 2 minutes per side, or until heated throughout. Remove from heat and serve immediately.

Makes 4 servings

Mini Lemon Sandwich Bites

1 C. plus 1½ T. butter, softened, divided
½ C. powdered sugar
2 C. flour
2½ tsp. lemon zest, divided
½ tsp. salt
1 egg, beaten
⅔ C. sugar
3 T. lemon juice

In a medium bowl, cream together 1 cup butter and powdered sugar. Stir in the flour, 1 teaspoon lemon zest and salt. Mix until well combined, cover and chill in refrigerator for 1 hour.

Preheat oven to 400°. Remove dough from refrigerator. Place teaspoonfuls of dough on ungreased baking sheets. Flatten each dough ball into a small circle and bake for about 5 to 8 minutes, until just lightly browned. Remove cookies to racks to cool.

To prepare filling, in a double boiler over boiling water, combine beaten egg, sugar, lemon juice, remaining 1½ teaspoons lemon zest and remaining 1½ tablespoons butter. Mix until well combined and stir until thickened. Place about 1 teaspoon of the filling over half of the cookies. Top with remaining cookies to form sandwiches. Store in an airtight container until ready to serve.

Makes about 24 servings

Mint Chocolate Sandwich Cookies

Ingredients

¼ C. plus 6 T. butter, divided
1½ C. brown sugar
2 T. water
2 C. semi-sweet chocolate chips
2 eggs
1 tsp. vanilla
2½ C. flour
1½ tsp. baking soda
1 tsp. salt
2½ C. powdered sugar
3 T. milk
½ tsp. peppermint extract
3 drops green food coloring

Directions

In a medium saucepan over low heat, combine 6 tablespoons butter, brown sugar, water and chocolate chips. Heat, stirring often, until chocolate is completely melted. Remove from heat and let cool. Use a wire whisk to beat in the eggs and vanilla.

In a medium bowl, combine the flour, baking soda and 1 teaspoon salt; mix well. Slowly stir flour mixture into the chocolate. Drop teaspoonfuls of the dough 2″ apart on an ungreased baking sheet. Bake in oven for 10 to 12 minutes, or until firm. Remove cookies to wire racks to cool.

In a separate bowl, combine powdered sugar, remaining ¼ cup butter, milk, peppermint extract, green food coloring and a pinch of salt. Mix until smooth. Spread mint filling over half of the cooled cookies. Top with remaining cookies to form sandwiches. Store in an airtight container until ready to serve.

Makes about 15 servings

Index

Index

Index

Index

"Sandwiches are wonderful.
You don't need a spoon or a plate!"
— Paul Lynde